COPING
WITH
ANXIETY

10 simple ways to relieve anxiety, fear & worry

EDMUND BOURNE, PH.D.
& LORNA GARANO

New Harbinger Publications, Inc.

Publisher's Note

Distributed in Canada by Raincoast Books.

Copyright © 2003 by Edmund J. Bourne and Lorna Garano
New Harbinger Publications, Inc.
5674 Shattuck Avenue
Oakland, CA 94609

Cover design by Amy Shoup
Text design by Michele Waters

ISBN 1-57224-320-1 Paperback

Printed in the United States of America

New Harbinger Publications' Web site address:
www.newharbinger.com

06   05   04
10 9 8 7 6

For all who seek to find a more peaceful way to live
—Ed Bourne

For my parents
—Lorna Garano

Contents

Preface

Anxiety is increasingly prevalent in modern society. Approximately 15 percent of the population of the United States, or nearly 40 million people, have suffered from an anxiety disorder in the past year. Why is anxiety so common in our time? Is there something about contemporary society that especially promotes anxiety? Throughout history people have been exposed to challenging events in the form of wars, famines, plagues, and disease. Yet anxiety seems to be particularly characteristic of our modern era. What's wrong?

In trying to account for the current prevalence of anxiety, at least three factors might be cited: the pace of modern life, a general lack of consensus about standards and values to live by, and the level of social alienation fostered by postindustrial society.

The pace of modern life has increased dramatically in recent decades. Films of people from fifty years ago show conclusively that people walked, drove, and lived more slowly than they do at present. Most of us live our lives in a state of constant doing, at odds with the natural rhythms of our bodies. Deprived of rest and time to just let ourselves "be," we become detached from ourselves and more anxious.

Along with the rapid pace of daily life, we all face an unprecedented pace of social, technological, and environmental change. Our environment and social order have changed more in the past fifty years than they did in the preceding three hundred years. The rate of change is only likely to increase in the future. Without adequate time to assimilate and adjust to all of this change, we find ourselves growing more anxious.

Norms in modern life are highly pluralistic. There is no shared, consistent, socially-agreed-upon set of values and standards for people to live by, as there tended to be prior to 1960. In the vacuum left, most of us attempt to fend for ourselves, and the resultant uncertainty about how to conduct our lives leaves ample room for anxiety. Faced with a barrage of inconsistent world views and standards presented by the media, we are left with the responsibility of having to create our own meaning and moral order. When we are unable to find that meaning, many of us are prone to fill the gap that's left with various forms of escapism and addiction. We tend live out of tune with ourselves and thus find ourselves anxious.

Security and stability arise through *connection:* feeling connected to someone or something outside of yourself. Anxiety arises in the moment when you lose your sense of connection—to yourself, others, your community, nature, or perhaps your God or Higher Power. When you feel disconnected or alienated, you're more prone to perceive something—almost anything—as a potential threat to your security and well-being. If you look for the roots of anxiety in modern life, much of it appears to arise from *a perception of threat in the absence of feeling connected.*

Our present way of life in postindustrial society contributes in many ways to feelings of alienation and disconnection. Historically, people lived in intimate connection with nature. Contrast this with modern life, where we commute on freeways to get to work, eat processed food and wear clothes manufactured thousands of miles away, and spend a great deal of our time in front of TV or computer screens. One hundred years ago people knew their neighbors and members of their immediate community. Today, we live in single-family homes and apartment complexes where often we are barely acquainted with those around us. We may be so involved in our own lives that we become oblivious to (or threatened by) strangers who might need our help. In our great-grandparents' era (and in some third-world countries at present), children were raised in the context of an extended family. Contrast this with modern society where we often move away from parents and siblings, raising our children in isolated nuclear families. And with the divorce rate at 50 percent, the nuclear family is often split, with children being shuttled back and forth.

The list could go on. Many of us are separated from our own hearts and souls by a variety of addictions ranging from alcohol and drugs to work, caretaking, or money and material goods. We are flooded with media images exhorting us to be perfect (or that we will be perfect if we buy the "right" item), reinforcing values of consumerism, materialism, and instant gratification that only serve to amplify the void many of us feel in our lives. Even our health-care system has become strictly profit oriented, with corporate HMOs cutting back on benefits, allowable tests, psychological treatment, and other services in order to protect the interests of their shareholders. All of these trends tend to aggravate our sense of insecurity, alienation, and feelings of insignificance. Add to this the steady threat of unprovoked terrorist attacks, and the picture is complete. We simply live in anxious times. Is it any wonder that anxiety is becoming increasingly prevalent?

An old saying advises: "It is better to light a candle than curse the darkness." Since outer society and the media offer little refuge, it is necessary for each of us to ask what we can do for ourselves. Many of us are looking for solutions, simple ways that we can make our lives more peaceful and livable. This book strives to provide some help in that direction. Our aim here is to provide you with an array of simple tools to help you find greater calm and stability in the midst of complex, even chaotic times. By finding ways to relieve anxiety and create peace in your own life, you not only benefit yourself but become a helpful role model to those around you.

Introduction

This is a book about how to cope with anxiety. Anxiety is an experience familiar to nearly everyone, and it seems increasingly prevalent amid the many stresses and complexities of modern life. About 25 percent of the adult population in the United States has a serious problem with anxiety at some time in their life.

Practical strategies are offered here to help you better handle your anxiety in all its forms. Before proceeding with these strategies, though, you may want to know a little more about the nature of anxiety itself. Anxiety comes in many shapes and sizes. Understanding the particular type—as well as the severity—of your own issue with anxiety (for example, everyday anxiety versus a particular anxiety disorder) will help you to get a better idea of what you're dealing with. Beyond this, it is also useful to know something about the diverse causes of anxiety. Understanding where your particular issues with anxiety might have come from—and especially what causes are likely to keep it going—will give you some reference points to determine which of the many strategies offered in this book might be most helpful.

Varieties of Anxiety

You can better understand the nature of anxiety by looking at both what it is and what it is not. For example, anxiety can be distinguished from fear in several ways. When you are afraid, your fear is usually directed toward some concrete, external object or situation that is immediately present. You might fear not meeting a deadline, failing an exam, or being rejected by someone you want to please. When you experience anxiety, on the other hand, you frequently can't specify what it is you're anxious about.

Rather than fearing a specific object or situation, you may imagine some danger that is not immediately present and only remotely likely. You may be anxious about the future, about your overall safety or security, or about going forward in the face of uncertainty. Or you might be anxious about losing control of yourself or some situation. Or you might feel a vague anxiety about something bad happening when you face a specific challenge.

Anxiety affects your whole being. It is a physiological, behavioral, and psychological reaction all at once. On a *physiological* level, anxiety may include bodily reactions such as rapid heartbeat, muscle tension, queasiness, dry mouth, or sweating. On a *behavioral* level, it can paralyze your ability to act, express yourself, or deal with certain everyday situations. *Psychologically*, anxiety is a subjective state of apprehension and uneasiness. In its most extreme form, it can cause you to feel detached from yourself and even fearful of dying or going crazy.

The fact that anxiety can affect you on physiological, behavioral, and psychological levels has important implications for your attempts to cope. A complete program of coping with anxiety must address all three components. You need to learn how to reduce physiological reactivity, eliminate avoidance behavior, and change self-talk that perpetuates a state of apprehension and worry.

Anxiety can appear in different forms and at different levels of intensity. It can range in severity from a mere twinge of uneasiness to a full-blown panic attack marked by heart palpitations, trembling, sweating, dizziness, disorientation, and terror. Anxiety that is not connected with any particular situation, that comes out of the blue, is called "free-floating anxiety" or, in more severe instances, a spontaneous "panic attack."

If your anxiety arises only in response to a specific situation, it is called "situational anxiety" or "phobic anxiety." *Situational anxiety* is different from everyday worries in that it tends to be out of proportion or unrealistic. If you have a disproportionate apprehension about driving on freeways, going to the doctor, or socializing, this may qualify as situational anxiety. Situational anxiety becomes *phobic* when you actually start to *avoid* the situation: if you give up driving on freeways, going to doctors, or socializing altogether. In other words, phobic anxiety is situational anxiety that includes persistent avoidance of the situation.

Often anxiety can be brought on merely by thinking about a particular situation. When you feel distressed about what might happen when you have to face a difficult or even phobic situation, you are experiencing what is called *anticipatory anxiety*. In its milder forms, anticipatory anxiety is indistinguishable from ordinary worry. Worrying can be defined as anticipating unpleasant consequences about a future situation. But sometimes anticipatory anxiety becomes intense enough to be *anticipatory panic*.

There is an important difference between spontaneous anxiety (or panic) and anticipatory anxiety (or panic). Spontaneous anxiety tends to come out of the blue, peaks to a high level very rapidly, and then subsides gradually. The peak is usually reached within five minutes, followed by a gradual tapering-off period of up to an hour or more. Anticipatory anxiety, on the other hand, tends to build up more gradually in response to encountering or simply thinking about a threatening situation, and may last longer. You may worry yourself into a frenzy about something for an hour or more and then let go of the worry as you tire or find something else to occupy your mind.

Anxiety versus Anxiety Disorders

Anxiety is an inevitable part of life in contemporary society. It's important to realize that there are many situations that come up in everyday life where it's appropriate and reasonable to react with some anxiety. If you didn't feel any anxiety in response to everyday challenges involving potential loss or failure, something would be wrong. This book can be of use to anyone experiencing normal, ordinary anxiety reactions (everyone, in other words) as well as those dealing with specific anxiety disorders. Incorporating exercise, relaxation skills, and good nutritional habits into your daily life—as well as paying attention to self-talk, mistaken beliefs, self-nurturing, and simplifying your lifestyle—can all help to make your life less anxious, regardless of the nature and extent of the anxiety you happen to be dealing with.

Seven Major Anxiety Disorders

Anxiety disorders are distinguished from everyday, normal anxiety in that they involve anxiety that is *more intense* (for example, panic attacks), *lasts longer* (anxiety that may persist for months instead of going away after a stressful situation has passed), or *leads to phobias* that interfere with your life. The following are recognized by mental health professionals as specific anxiety disorders.

Panic Disorder

Panic disorder is marked by sudden episodes of acute, intense anxiety that appear to come out of the blue. You have at least one such attack per month and worry about having additional attacks some of the time. Often panic attacks are accompanied by irrational fears such as the fear of heart attack, sudden illness, or going crazy. To the person in its grip, panic can be terrifying.

Agoraphobia

Agoraphobia is characterized by a fear of panic attacks in situations that are perceived to be far from safety or a safe place (such as home), or from which escape might be difficult (such as driving on a freeway or waiting in line at the grocery store). Such fear can lead to avoidance of a wide range of situations.

Social Phobia

Social phobia is an exaggerated fear of embarrassment or humiliation in situations where you are exposed to the scrutiny of others or must perform. It's often accompanied by partial or total avoidance of the situation. You may be fearful of attending meetings at work, speaking up in class, going to parties or social outings, meeting new people, or even using public restrooms. The fear can take many forms.

Specific Phobia

Specific phobia is a strong fear and avoidance of *one* particular object or situation (such as spiders, water, thunderstorms, elevators, or flying).

Generalized Anxiety Disorder

Generalized anxiety disorder involves chronic anxiety and worry for at least six months about two or more issues or activities (such as work or health). Physiological symptoms such as muscle tension and rapid heartbeat are common. No panic attacks or phobias are present.

Obsessive-Compulsive Disorder

Obsessive-compulsive disorder is characterized by recurring obsessions (repetitive thoughts) that won't leave your mind and/or compulsions (rituals performed to dispel anxiety) that are severe enough to be time-consuming or cause marked distress. Persistent handwashing or repetitive checking are two common types of this problem.

Post-Traumatic Stress Disorder

Post-traumatic stress disorder involves anxiety and other persistent symptoms (such as flashbacks and emotional numbing) following an acute and intense trauma (such as a natural disaster, assault, rape, or accident). It can also occur after witnessing an event that involves death or injury to another person.

Criteria for diagnosing specific anxiety disorders have been established by the American Psychiatric Association and are listed in a well-known diagnostic manual used by mental health professionals called DSM-IV (Diagnostic and Statistical Manual of Mental Disorders). For more detailed descriptions of each of the anxiety disorders, along with specific guidelines for their treatment, see chapter 1 of *The Anxiety and Phobia Workbook* (Bourne 2000).

Causes of Anxiety

Anxiety symptoms often seem irrational and inexplicable, so it's only natural to raise the question, why?

Before considering in detail the various causes of anxiety, there are two general points you should bear in mind. First, although learning about the causes of anxiety can give you insight into how anxiety problems develop, such knowledge is unnecessary to overcome your particular difficulty. The various strategies for handling anxiety presented in this book, such as relaxation, realistic thinking, desensitization, exercise, nutrition, and self-nurturing, do not depend on a knowledge of underlying causes to be effective. However much you may know about causes, this knowledge is not necessarily what cures.

Second, be wary of the notion that there is one primary cause, or type of cause, for either everyday anxiety or anxiety disorders. Whether you are dealing with ordinary anxiety, apprehension about a job interview, panic disorder, or obsessive-compulsive disorder, recognize that there is no one cause which, if removed, would eliminate the problem. Anxiety problems are brought about by a variety of causes operating on numerous levels. These levels include heredity, biology, family background and upbringing, conditioning, recent life changes, your self-talk and personal belief system, your ability to express feelings, current environmental stressors, and so on.

Some experts in the field of anxiety disorders propose single-cause theories. Such theories tend to greatly oversimplify anxiety disorders and are susceptible to one of two mistaken lines of reasoning: the *biological fallacy* and the *psychological fallacy*.

The biological fallacy assumes that a particular type of anxiety disorder is caused solely by some biological or physiological imbalance in the brain or body. For example, there has recently been a tendency to reduce the causation of panic disorder, as well as obsessive-compulsive disorder, to a strictly biological level—some kind of imbalance in the brain. It's helpful to know that there may be brain dysfunctions involved in anxiety, and particularly anxiety disorders. This certainly has implications for treatment of these problems. But this does not mean that anxiety and anxiety disorders are physiological disturbances only. The question remains: what caused the physiological disturbance itself? Perhaps chronic stress due to psychological conflict or repressed anger causes specific brain imbalances that lead to difficulties such as panic attacks or generalized anxiety disorder. Psychological conflicts and repressed anger may, in turn, have been caused in large part by a person's upbringing. Because any particular brain disturbance may have originally been set up by stress or other psychological factors, it is a fallacy to assume that anxiety and anxiety disorders are *solely* (or even primarily) caused by physiological imbalances.

The psychological fallacy makes the same kind of mistake in the opposite direction. It assumes that, say, social phobia or generalized anxiety disorder is caused by having grown up with parents who neglected, abandoned, or abused you, resulting in a deep-seated sense of insecurity or shame that causes your current phobic avoidance and anxiety as an adult. While it may be true that your family background contributed in an important way to your current problems, is it reasonable to assume that this is the *only* cause? Again, not really. To do so overlooks the possible contributions of hereditary and biological factors. After all, not all children who grow up in dysfunctional families develop anxiety disorders. And children growing up with good parenting may still develop anxiety difficulties. Many problems with anxiety, particularly more severe problems with anxiety disorders, are a result of both a hereditary predisposition toward anxiety and early childhood conditions that fostered a sense of shame or insecurity. Anxiety problems are also likely related to a variety of factors in your current lifestyle, as well as recent stress you've experienced.

In sum, the idea that your particular difficulties are just a brain imbalance or just a psychological disturbance neglects the fact that nature and nurture are interactive. While brain imbalances may certainly be set up by heredity, they may also result from stress or psychological factors. Psychological problems, in turn, may be influenced by inborn biological predispositions. There is simply no way to say which came first or which is the "ultimate" cause. By the same token, a comprehensive approach to overcoming anxiety, panic, worry, or phobias cannot restrict itself to treating physiological or psychological causes in isolation. A variety of strategies dealing with several different levels—including biological, behavioral, emotional, mental, interpersonal, and even spiritual factors—are necessary. This multidimensional approach to overcoming anxiety is assumed throughout this book.

The causes of anxiety difficulties vary not only according to the level at which they occur, but also according to the *time period* over which they operate. The following describes some typical causes that begin at various times in life.

Long-Term, Predisposing Causes

These are conditions that set you up from birth or childhood to develop anxiety difficulties later on. They include heredity, dysfunctional parenting, or early trauma or abuse (for example, parental neglect, rejection, overcriticism, overpunishment, overcautiousness, alcoholism, or physical and/or sexual abuse).

Recent Circumstantial Causes

These are events that trigger the onset of, say, panic attacks or agoraphobia. They include a heightened level of stress over the past month or two (or an accumulation of stress over a longer time period), significant loss, significant life change (for example, a major move, starting a new job, getting married), illness, or recreational drug use (especially cocaine, amphetamines, or marijuana).

Maintaining Causes

These are factors in your current behavior, attitude, and lifestyle that keep anxiety going once it has developed. Maintaining causes are manifold and include muscle tension; fearful self-talk ("what-if" thinking); mistaken beliefs about self, others, or life; continued avoidance of fear or fearful situations; lack of movement and exercise; caffeine, sugar, and junk food consumption; lack of self-nurturing skills; excessively complicated lifestyle and environment; indulging the "habit" of worry; and low self-confidence and self-worth (feeling you are a "victim" rather than empowered to "take charge" of anxiety).

Neurobiological Causes

These are conditions in your brain that immediately affect the course and intensity of your current experience of anxiety. They include:

- Deficiencies or imbalances in certain neurotransmitters, particularly serotonin, norepinephrine, and GABA

- Excessive reactivity of certain brain structures, especially the amygdala and locus ceruleus

- Insufficient inhibition or "braking" of excessive reactivity by higher brain centers such as the frontal or temporal cortex

See chapter 2 of *The Anxiety and Phobia Workbook* for a more detailed account of the brain imbalances that influence anxiety (Bourne 2000).

Help for Maintaining Causes

This book primarily addresses the third group of causes, the maintaining causes of anxiety. All of the maintaining causes mentioned above, and several others, will be considered. What you'll learn from this book will also affect the neurobiological causes (mind, behavior, and brain are all interactive), but more indirectly. The long-term, predisposing causes are more difficult to change. Short of genetic engineering and direct modification of your DNA structure (a distinct possibility in the future), you cannot change your genes. However, you can certainly change the way you respond to and deal with your genetic predispositions. This book will help you to do this. In regard to dysfunctional parenting, you can't change what happened to you as a child. However, you can learn about and work through the effects of a traumatic or abusive childhood by reading books on the subject (see the Resources section) and especially by obtaining psychotherapy from a qualified therapist.

Recent, circumstantial causes of your difficulties with anxiety have already happened. However, utilizing the strategies in this book will help you to better deal with recent as well as long-term stresses that you've encountered. Managing the stress in your life—past, recent, or present—will go a long way to help you better cope with everyday anxiety, worry, or specific anxiety disorders.

The Role of Medications

One intervention not covered in this book is medication. It's the intention of this book to present an array of easy-to-use, state-of-the-art coping strategies for overcoming anxiety. Since use of prescription medications is not really a self-help technique, but relies on the expertise of a physician, it has not been included. However, prescription medications are widely used in helping people with anxiety, especially those persons struggling with more severe cases of anxiety disorders such as panic disorder, agoraphobia, obsessive-compulsive disorder, and post-traumatic stress disorder. Because medications are commonly used to help people with anxiety disorders, they deserve a special note.

The use of medication is a critical issue among those who struggle with anxiety on a daily basis, as well as for professionals treating anxiety disorders. Generalizations about the use of medication are difficult to make. The pros and cons of relying on medication are unique and variable in each individual case. For everyday anxiety and worry, prescription drugs are usually unnecessary. Normal and mild forms of anxiety yield to natural methods. Quite a few people find that they can avoid drugs—or eliminate those they have been taking—by implementing a comprehensive wellness program that includes simplifying their life and environment to reduce stress; making ample time for rest and relaxation; regular aerobic exercise; positive changes in nutrition and use of appropriate supplements; changes in self-talk and basic beliefs (encouraging a less driven, more relaxed approach to life); and support from family and friends.

Such approaches may be all you need if your anxiety symptoms are relatively mild. "Mild" means that your problem does not significantly interfere with your ability to work or your important relationships. Also, the problem does not cause you serious or constant distress.

If, on the other hand, you have a more severe problem with anxiety, appropriate use of medication may be an important part of your treatment. This is particularly true if you are dealing with panic disorder, agoraphobia, severe forms of social phobia, obsessive-compulsive disorder, or post-traumatic stress disorder. "Severe" means your anxiety is disruptive enough that it's difficult for you to get to work or function on your job (or it has caused you to stop working). It also means that your anxiety causes you distress at least 50 percent of the time you are awake. It's not just a nuisance or irritation—you often feel overwhelmed by it.

If you believe your anxiety problem falls into the moderate-to-severe range, you may benefit from trying a medication such as an SSRI (selective serotonin reuptake inhibitor) like Paxil, Zoloft, Celexa, or Luvox. Other medications like Buspar or Neurontin may also be helpful. Not trying medications because you are afraid or philosophically opposed to them may actually hamper your recovery if your situation is severe. When anxiety is severe and disruptive, it's often important to relieve it with medication early before it gains a foothold and becomes more chronic. On the other hand, if your anxiety is in the mild-to-moderate range, you can probably overcome it on your own using the methods described in this book.

More detailed guidelines for when to use medication and which ones to use can be found in chapter 17 of *The Anxiety and Phobia Workbook* (Bourne 2000). You can also obtain a referral to a psychiatrist in your area skilled in treating anxiety disorders by contacting the Anxiety Disorders Association of America at (240) 485-1001 or going to their web site (www.adaa.org) and clicking on "Find a Therapist."

Relax Your Body

By the end of this chapter ...
  You will know how to:

- Recognize the muscle tension that contributes to anxiety
- Progressively or passively relax your muscles to diffuse anxiety when it hits
- Use cue-controlled relaxation
- Recognize the breathing patterns that fuel anxiety
- Use abdominal breathing to control your anxiety symptoms, such as hyperventilation and shortness of breath
- Get started on a yoga routine

It's All in Your Head ... and Arms, and Feet, and Legs, and Hands

Anxiety often manifests itself as a cluster of physical symptoms. In fact, when asked to describe their anxiety many people begin by enumerating a list of disquieting physical sensations, such as shortness of breath, muscle tension, hyperventilation, and palpitations. Such symptoms reinforce anxiety-producing thoughts. Try to think for a moment of your anxiety as a solely physical condition. What are the symptoms of this condition? How do they affect your sense of well-being? How do you respond to them? Although it may seem like these physical symptoms are automatic reflexes beyond your control, you can take comfort in knowing that they are not. With practice, you can stem the physical effects of anxiety and free yourself from its grip.

Progressive Muscle Relaxation

Progressive muscle relaxation is a simple technique used to halt anxiety by relaxing your muscles one group at a time. Its effectiveness was recognized decades ago by Edmund Jacobson, a Chicago physician. In 1929 he published what has become a classic, *Progressive Relaxation*. In it he described this deep muscle relaxation technique which, he asserted, required no imagination, willpower, or suggestion. His technique is based on the premise that the body responds to anxiety-inducing thoughts with muscle tension. This muscle tension then induces more anxiety and triggers a vicious cycle. Stop the muscle tension, stop the cycle. "An anxious mind cannot exist in a relaxed body," Dr. Jacobson once said.

"I'm Uptight"

If your anxiety is strongly associated with muscle tension, progressive muscle relaxation will probably prove an especially useful tool for you. This muscle tension is often what leads you to say that you are "uptight" or "tense." You may experience chronic tightness in your shoulders and neck, for example, which can be effectively relieved by practicing progressive muscle relaxation. Other symptoms that respond well to progressive muscle relaxation include tension headaches, backaches, tightness in the jaw, tightness around the eyes, muscle spasms, high blood pressure, and insomnia. If you are troubled by racing thoughts, you may find that systematically relaxing your muscles tends to slow down your mind. If you take tranquilizers, you may find that regular practice of progressive muscle relaxation will enable you to lower your dosage.

If You've Suffered an Injury

There are no contraindications for progressive muscle relaxation unless the muscle groups to be tensed and relaxed have been injured. If this is the case, consult your doctor before attempting progressive muscle relaxation.

Progressive Muscle Relaxation Technique

Progressive muscle relaxation involves tensing and relaxing, in succession, sixteen different muscle groups of the body. The idea is to tense each muscle group hard (but not so hard that you strain it) for about ten seconds, and then to let go of it suddenly. Then you give yourself fifteen to twenty seconds to relax, noticing how the muscle group feels when relaxed in contrast to how it felt when tensed, before going on to the next group of muscles.

Some Guidelines for Practicing Progressive Muscle Relaxation

Practice at least twenty minutes per day. Two twenty-minute periods are optimal. One daily twenty-minute session is mandatory for obtaining generalization effects. "Generalization" means that the relaxation you experience during progressive muscle relaxation spreads or "generalizes" to the rest of your day, or at least for several hours, after you've been practicing daily for two or three weeks. You may want to begin your practice with thirty-minute periods. As you gain skill in this relaxation technique, you will find that the amount of time you need to experience the relaxation response will decrease.

Find a quiet location to practice where you won't be distracted. This is crucial. Don't permit the phone to ring while you're practicing. Use a fan or air conditioner to block out background noise if necessary.

Practice at regular times. Generally, on awakening, before retiring, or before meals are the best times. A consistent daily relaxation routine will increase the likelihood of generalization effects.

Practice on an empty stomach. Food digestion after meals will tend to disrupt deep relaxation.

Assume a comfortable position. Your entire body, including your head, should be supported. Lying down on a sofa or bed or sitting in a reclining chair are two ways of supporting your body most completely. (When lying down, you may want to place a pillow beneath your knees for further support.) Sitting up is preferable to lying down if you are feeling tired and sleepy. It's advantageous to experience the full depth of the relaxation response consciously without going to sleep.

Let your body be unencumbered. Loosen any tight garments and take off shoes, watch, glasses, contact lenses, jewelry, and so on.

Make a decision not to worry about anything. Give yourself permission to put aside the concerns of the day. Allow taking care of yourself and having peace of mind to take precedence over any of your worries. *Success with relaxation depends on giving peace of mind high priority in your overall scheme of values.*

Assume a passive, detached attitude. This is probably the most important element. You want to adopt a "let it happen" attitude and be free of any worry about how well you are performing the technique: Do not try to relax; do not try to control your body; do not judge your performance. The point is to let go.

Tense, don't strain. When you tense a particular muscle group, do so vigorously, without straining, for seven to ten seconds. You may want to count one-thousand-one, one-thousand-two, and so on, as a way of marking off seconds.

Concentrate on what is happening. Feel the buildup of tension in each particular muscle group. It is often helpful to visualize the particular muscle group being tensed.

Let go. When you release a particular muscle group, do so abruptly, and then relax, enjoying the sudden feeling of limpness. Allow relaxation to develop for at least fifteen to twenty seconds before going on to the next group of muscles.

Try repeating a relaxing phrase. You might say to yourself "I am relaxing," "let go," "let the tension flow away," or any other relaxing phrase, during each relaxation period between successive muscle groups.

Maintain your focus on your muscles. Throughout the exercise you should keep focused on your muscles. When your attention wanders, bring it back to the particular muscle group you're working on.

Exercise: Progressive Muscle Relaxation

Once you are comfortably supported in a quiet place, follow the steps below.

1. To begin, take three deep abdominal breaths, exhaling slowly each time. As you exhale, imagine the tension throughout your body beginning to flow away.

2. Clench your fists. Hold for seven to ten seconds and then release for fifteen to twenty seconds. Use these same time intervals for all other muscle groups.

3. Tighten your biceps by drawing your forearms up toward your shoulders and making a muscle with both arms. Hold ... and then relax.

4. Tighten your triceps, the muscles on the undersides of your upper arms, by extending your arms out straight and locking your elbows. Hold ... and then relax.

5. Tense the muscles in your forehead by raising your eyebrows as far as you can. Hold ... and then relax. Imagine your forehead muscles becoming smooth and limp as they relax.

6. Tense the muscles around your eyes by clenching your eyelids tightly shut. Hold ... and then relax. Imagine sensations of deep relaxation spreading all around the area of your eyes.

7. Tighten your jaws by opening your mouth so widely that you stretch the muscles around the hinges of your jaw. Hold ... and then relax. Let your lips part and allow your jaw to hang loose.

8. Tighten the muscles in the back of your neck by pulling your head way back, as if you were going to touch your head to your back (be gentle with this muscle group to avoid injury). Focus only on tensing the muscles in your neck. Hold ... and then relax. Since this area is often especially tight, it's good to do this tense-relax cycle twice.

9. Take a few deep breaths and tune in to the weight of your head sinking into whatever surface it is resting on.

10. Tighten your shoulders by raising them up as if you were going to touch your ears. Hold ... and then relax.

11. Tighten the muscles around your shoulder blades by pushing your shoulder blades back as if you were going to touch them together. Hold the tension in your shoulder blades ... and then relax. Since this area is often especially tense, you might repeat this tense-relax sequence twice.

12. Tighten the muscles of your chest by taking in a deep breath. Hold for up to ten seconds ... and then

release slowly. Imagine any excess tension in your chest flowing away with the exhalation.

13. Tighten your stomach muscles by sucking your stomach in. Hold ... and then release. Imagine a wave of relaxation spreading through your abdomen.

14. Tighten your lower back by arching it up. (You can omit this exercise if you have lower back pain.) Hold ... and then relax.

15. Tighten your buttocks by pulling them together. Hold ... and then relax. Imagine the muscles in your hips going loose and limp.

16. Squeeze the muscles in your thighs all the way down to your knees. You will probably have to tighten your hips along with your thighs, since the thigh muscles attach at the pelvis. Hold ... and then relax. Feel your thigh muscles smoothing out and relaxing completely.

17. Tighten your calf muscles by pulling your toes toward you (flex carefully to avoid cramps). Hold ... and then relax.

18. Tighten your feet by curling your toes downward. Hold ... and then relax.

19. Mentally scan your body for any residual tension. If a particular area remains tense, repeat one or two tense-relax cycles for that group of muscles.

20. Now imagine a wave of relaxation slowly spreading throughout your body, starting at your head and gradually penetrating every muscle group all the way down to your toes.

The entire progressive muscle relaxation sequence should take you twenty to thirty minutes the first time. With practice you may decrease the time needed to fifteen to twenty minutes. You might want to record the above exercises on an audio cassette to expedite your early practice sessions. Or you may wish to obtain a professionally made tape of the progressive muscle relaxation exercise. Some people always prefer to use a tape, while others have the exercises so well learned after a few weeks of practice that they prefer doing them from memory.

Passive Muscle Relaxation

As an alternative to progressive muscle relaxation you may want to try passive muscle relaxation, which does not require actively tensing and relaxing your muscles. Progressive muscle relaxation is a bit more "potent medicine" for body tension, but passive muscle relaxation works quite well too.

Exercise: Passive Muscle Relaxation

Start out by taking two or three deep breaths ... and let yourself settle back into the chair, the bed, or wherever you happen to be right now ... making yourself fully comfortable. Let this be a time just for you, putting aside all worries and concerns of the day ... and making this a time just for you ... letting each part of your body begin to relax ... starting with your feet. Just imagine your feet letting go and relaxing right now ... letting go of any excess tension in your feet. Just imagine it draining away ... and as your feet are relaxing, imagine relaxation moving up into your calves. Let the muscles in your calves unwind and loosen up and let go ... allow any tension you're feeling in your calves to just drain away easily and quickly ... and as your calves are relaxing, allow relaxation to move up into your thighs ... Let the muscles in your thighs unwind and smooth out and relax completely. You might begin to feel your legs from your waist down to your feet becoming more and more relaxed. You might notice your legs becoming heavy as they relax more and more. Continuing now to let the relaxation move into your hips ... feeling any excess tension in your hips dissolve and flow away. And soon you might allow relaxation to move into your stomach area ... just letting go of any strain or discomfort in your stomach ... let it all go right now, imagining deep sensations of relaxation spreading all around your stomach ... and continuing to allow the relaxation to move up into your chest. All the muscles in your chest can unwind and loosen up and let go. Each time you exhale, you might imagine breathing away any remaining tension in your chest until your chest feels completely relaxed ... and you find it easy to enjoy the good feeling of relaxation as it deepens and develops throughout your chest, stomach area, and your legs. And shortly, you might allow relaxation to move into your shoulders ... just letting deep sensations of calmness and relaxation spread all through the muscles of your shoulders ... allowing your shoulders to drop ... allowing them to feel completely relaxed. And you might now allow the relaxation in your shoulders to move down into your arms, spreading into your upper arms, down into your elbows and forearms, and finally all the way down to your wrists and hands ... letting your arms relax ... enjoying the good feeling of relaxation in your arms ... putting aside any worries, any uncomfortable, unpleasant thoughts right now ... letting yourself be totally in the present moment as you let yourself relax more and more. You can feel relaxation moving into your neck now. All the muscles in your neck just unwind, smooth out, and

relax completely. Imagine the muscles in your neck
loosening up just like a knotted cord being unraveled.
And soon, the relaxation can move into your chin
and jaws ... allowing your jaws to relax ... letting
your jaws loosen up, and as they are relaxing, you
can imagine relaxation moving into the area around
your eyes. Any tension around your eyes can just
dissipate and flow away as you allow your eyes to
relax completely. Any eyestrain just dissolves now
and your eyes can fully relax. And you let your
forehead relax too ... letting the muscles in your
forehead smooth out and relax completely ... noticing
the weight of your head against whatever it's resting on
as you allow your entire head to relax completely. Just
enjoying the good feeling of relaxation all over now ...
letting yourself drift deeper and deeper into quietness
and peace ... getting more and more in touch with that
place deep inside of perfect stillness and serenity.

Relaxation without Tension

As you continue to practice progressive muscle relaxation you
will become more adept at recognizing and releasing tension in
your muscles. In fact, you may become so attuned to what's happening in your body that you need not deliberately contract each
muscle before you relax it. Instead, scan your body for tension by
running your attention through this sequence of four muscle
groups: arms, head and neck, shoulders and torso, and legs. If
you find any tightness, simply let go of it, just as you did after
each contraction in the progressive muscle relaxation exercise.
Stay focused and really feel each sensation. Work with each of
the four muscle groups until the muscles seem completely
relaxed. If you come to an area that feels tight and won't let go,
tighten that one muscle or muscle group and then release the

tension. Relaxation without tension is also a good way to relax sore muscles that you don't want to aggravate by overtensing.

Cue-Controlled Relaxation

In cue-controlled relaxation, you learn to relax your muscles whenever you want by combining a verbal suggestion with abdominal breathing. First, take a comfortable position, then release as much tension as you can using the relaxation-without-tension method. Focus on your belly as it moves in and out with each breath. Make breaths slow and rhythmic. With each breath let yourself become more and more relaxed. Now, on every inhalation say to yourself the words *breathe in,* and as you exhale, the word *relax.* Just keep saying to yourself, "Breathe in ... relax, breathe in ... relax," while letting go of tension throughout your body. Continue this practice for five minutes, repeating the key phrases with each breath.

The cue-controlled method teaches your body to associate the word *relax* with the feeling of relaxation. After you have practiced this technique for a while and the association is strong, you'll be able to relax your muscles anytime, anywhere, just by mentally repeating, "Breathe in ... relax," and by releasing any feelings of tightness throughout your body. Cue-controlled relaxation can give you stress relief in less than a minute.

Abdominal Breathing

Most of us don't think much about our breathing patterns and how they reflect and contribute to our emotional state. But the way you breathe directly reflects the level of tension you carry in your body and can aggravate or diminish your anxiety symptoms. If you are like many anxiety sufferers, you've experienced one or both of the following breathing problems:

- Breathing too high up in your chest with your breathing too shallow.

- Breathing rapidly or hyperventilation, which results in breathing out too much carbon dioxide relative to the amount of oxygen carried in your bloodstream.

Is your breath slow or rapid? Deep or shallow? Does it center around a point high in your chest or down in your abdomen? You might also take note of changes in your breathing pattern under stress compared to when you are more relaxed.

Chest Breathing versus Abdominal Breathing

Under tension, your breathing usually becomes shallow and rapid, and occurs high in the chest. Shallow, chest-level breathing, when rapid, can lead to hyperventilation. Hyperventilation, in turn, can cause physical symptoms associated with anxiety, such as light-headedness, dizziness, heart palpitations, or tingling sensations. When relaxed, you breathe more fully, more deeply, and from your abdomen. It's difficult to be tense and to breathe from your abdomen at the same time. By changing your breathing pattern from up in your chest to down in your abdomen (stomach area), you can reverse the cycle and transform your breathing into a built-in tool for anxiety control.

Abdominal breathing triggers a host of physiological transactions that promote relaxation and diminish anxiety. Listed below are some of the benefits of abdominal breathing that translate into greater relaxation and lowered anxiety.

- Increased oxygen supply to the brain and musculature.

- Stimulation of the parasympathetic nervous system. This branch of your autonomic nervous system promotes a state of calmness and quiescence. It works in a fashion exactly opposite to the sympathetic branch of your nervous system, which stimulates a state of emotional arousal and the very physiological reactions underlying panic or anxiety.

- Greater feelings of connectedness between your mind and body. Anxiety and worry tend to keep you up in your head. A few minutes of deep abdominal breathing will help bring you down into your whole body.

- More efficient excretion of bodily toxins. Many toxic substances in the body are excreted through the lungs.

- Improved concentration. If your mind is racing, it's difficult to focus your attention. Abdominal breathing helps to quiet your mind.

- Abdominal breathing by itself can trigger a relaxation response.

The exercises below will help you change your breathing pattern. By practicing them, you can achieve a state of deep relaxation in a short period of time. Just three minutes of practicing abdominal breathing or the calming breath exercise will usually induce a deep state of relaxation. Many people successfully use one or the other technique to abort a panic attack at its first stirrings. The techniques are also very helpful in diminishing anticipatory anxiety you may experience in advance of facing a fearful situation or in easing everyday worry.

Exercise: Abdominal Breathing

1. Note the level of tension you're feeling. Then place one hand on your abdomen right beneath your rib cage.

2. Inhale slowly and deeply through your nose into the bottom of your lungs; in other words, send the air as low down as you can. If you're breathing from your

abdomen, your hand should actually rise. Your chest should move only slightly while your abdomen expands.

3. When you've taken in a full breath, pause for a moment and then exhale slowly through your nose or mouth, depending on your preference. Be sure to exhale fully. As you exhale, allow your whole body to just let go (you might visualize your arms and legs going loose and limp like a rag doll).

4. Do ten slow, full abdominal breaths. Try to keep your breathing smooth and regular, without gulping in a big breath or letting your breath out all at once. It will help to slow down your breathing if you slowly count to four on the inhale and then slowly count to four on the exhale. Use this count to slow down your breathing for a few breaths, then let it go. Remember to pause briefly at the end of each inhalation.

5. After you've slowed down your breathing, count from twenty down to one, counting backwards one number with each exhalation. The process should go like this:
   Slow inhale ... Pause ... Slow exhale (count twenty)
   Slow inhale ... Pause ... Slow exhale (count nineteen)
   Slow inhale ... Pause ... Slow exhale (count eighteen)
   and so on down to one. If you start to feel light-headed while practicing abdominal breathing, stop for fifteen to twenty seconds and breathe in your normal way, then start again.

6. Extend the exercise if you wish by doing two or three sets of abdominal breaths, remembering to count backwards from twenty to one for each set. Five full minutes of abdominal breathing will have a pronounced effect in reducing anxiety or early symptoms of panic. Some people prefer to count from one to twenty instead. Feel free to do this if you wish.

Exercise: Calming Breath

The Calming Breath exercise* was adapted from the ancient discipline of yoga. It is a very efficient technique for achieving a deep state of relaxation quickly. This exercise interrupts the momentum of anxiety symptoms.

1. Breathing from your abdomen, inhale through your nose slowly to a count of five (count slowly "one ... two ... three ... four ... five" as you inhale).

2. Pause and hold your breath to a count of five.

3. Exhale slowly, through your nose or mouth, to a count of five (or more if it takes you longer). Be sure to exhale fully.

4. When you've exhaled completely, take two breaths in your normal rhythm, then repeat steps 1 through 3.

5. Keep up the exercise for at least three to five minutes. This should involve going through *at least* ten cycles of in-five, hold-five, out-five. As you continue the exercise, you may notice that you can count higher when you exhale than when you inhale. Allow these variations in your counting to occur, and just continue with the exercise for up to five minutes. Remember to take two normal breaths between each cycle. If you start to feel light-headed while practicing this exercise, stop and breathe normaly for thirty seconds and then start again. Throughout this exercise, keep your breathing smooth and regular, without gulping in breaths or breathing out suddenly.

6. Optional: Each time you exhale, you may wish to say "relax," "calm," "let go," or any other relaxing word

---

* The name "calming breath" was taken from an exercise by that name developed by Reid Wilson in *Don't Panic: Taking Control of Anxiety Attacks*. The steps presented here differ significantly from Wilson's exercise.

or phrase silently to yourself. Allow your whole body to let go as you do this. If you keep this up each time you practice, eventually just saying your relaxing word by itself will bring about a mild state of relaxation.

Consistency Counts

Practice the Abdominal Breathing or Calming Breath exercise for five to ten minutes twice per day for at least two weeks. If possible, find a regular time each day to do this so that your breathing exercise becomes a habit. Using these exercises, you can learn to reverse the physiological reactions underlying anxiety or panic.

Try Yoga

The word "yoga" means to yoke or unify. By definition, yoga seeks to promote unity of mind, body, and spirit. Although in the West yoga is usually thought of as a series of stretching exercises, it actually embraces a broad philosophy of life and an elaborate system for personal transformation. This system includes ethical precepts, a vegetarian diet, the familiar stretches or postures, specific practices for directing and controlling the breath, concentration practices, and deep meditation. Yoga postures, by themselves, provide a very effective means to increase fitness, flexibility, and relaxation. They can be practiced alone or with a group.

Many people find that yoga simultaneously increases energy and vitality while calming the mind. Yoga may be compared to progressive muscle relaxation, in that it involves holding the body in certain flexed positions for a few moments and then relaxing. Like vigorous exercise, yoga directly promotes mind-body integration. Each yoga posture reflects a mental attitude, whether that attitude is one of surrender, as in certain forward-bending poses, or of strengthening the will, as in a backward-bending pose. If you are interested in learning yoga, the best place to start is with a class at a local health club or community college. If such classes are unavailable in your area, try working with a yoga video at home. The popular magazine *Yoga Journal* offers many excellent yoga videos.

In recent years yoga has become a very popular method for reducing anxiety and stress. We recommend giving it a try.

Relax Your Mind

By the end of this chapter ...
You will know how to:

- Use guided visualization to calm your mind

- Use basic meditation techniques to be in the present instead of worrying about the future

- Begin to assemble a relaxing music collection

The Speed of Thought

From the time we awaken until we fall asleep, we are engaged in an almost constant mental bustle. Anxiety may accelerate this so that you feel like your mind is racing and you're bombarded with thoughts. This chapter introduces guided visualization and meditation techniques that you can use daily to calm your mind and center yourself in the here and now. If you're like many Westerners, the idea of maintaining a daily regimen designed to relax your mind and induce serenity may sound foreign to you. But some of these techniques have endured for centuries and are now practiced the world over. In brief, they work.

Mastering the simple exercises in this chapter can translate into an overall sense of tranquillity and a defense against anxiety.

Imagine That

Images are one of the ways our thoughts take shape. The mental images you visualize can affect your behavior or state of being in profound ways apart from your deliberate, conscious will. When you are in the throes of anxiety you may imagine yourself in dire circumstances or conjure up unsettling mental scenes. It can feel as though you've taken the lead role in an Alfred Hitchcock movie that's running on a continuous loop in your mind. The power of imagination has long been recognized and it is, no doubt, formidable. But you should know that while it can be a source of anxiety, imagination can also be a tool for relaxation.

Guided Visualization

Guided visualization is a method of deliberately using mental imagery to modify your behavior, the way you feel, and even your internal physiological state. You can consciously create visualizations or mental sense impressions as a preventative measure against anxiety. When you practice guided visualization, you will close your eyes and imagine yourself in a calming scenario. Taking on this new role in a mental movie designed to induce serenity rather than suspense can go a long way to reduce your anxiety symptoms. Below are two guided visualizations you can use to relax your mind when you feel tense or worried, or find your thoughts racing.

The key to using guided visualization successfully is to practice it when you are relaxed. Visualization itself is inherently relaxing, but you may find it helpful to relax your body using abdominal breathing for a minute or two before you begin to practice visualization (see chapter 1). When you are relaxed, you're able to experience the images more vividly, and thus they are likely to have a more profound effect. So that you have the optimal chance to relax, it is useful to record guided visualizations on tape either in your own voice or by asking someone else to make the recording (naturally, you should choose someone whose voice sounds pleasant to you). After you've gone through the visualization a number of times on tape, you may recall it so well that you can do it on your own, or you may prefer to continue using the tape indefinitely.

Guidelines for Practicing Guided Visualization

1. Get into a comfortable position, free of encumbrances and with your head supported.

2. Be sure that your environment is quiet and free from distractions.

3. Give yourself time to relax before undertaking a guided visualization. To this end, you can use progressive muscle relaxation or abdominal breathing for a few minutes before you start.

4. At the conclusion of your relaxing visualization, bring yourself back to an alert state of mind with the following statement (which you can record at the end of your visualization tape):

   "Now, in a moment you can begin to come back to an alert, wakeful state of mind. Pay attention as I count from one up to five. When I get up to five, you can open your eyes and feel awake, alert, and refreshed. One ... gradually beginning to come back to an alert, wakeful state. Two ... more and more awake. Three ... beginning to move your hands and feet as you become more alert. Four ... almost back to a fully alert state. And five ... opening your eyes now, finding yourself fully awake, alert, and refreshed."

5. After finishing with your visualization, get up and walk around a bit until you feel fully alert and grounded.

6. Allow at least ten minutes to pass before driving a car or engaging in any other activity that requires complex coordination.

Exercise: A Guided Visualization of the Beach

You're walking down a long wooden stairway to a beautiful, expansive beach. It looks almost deserted and stretches off into the distance as far as you can see. The sand is very fine and light ... almost white in appearance. You step onto the sand in your bare feet and rub it between your toes. It feels so good to walk slowly along this beautiful beach. The roaring sound of the surf is so soothing that you can just let go of anything on your mind. You're watching the waves ebb and flow ... they are slowly coming in ... breaking over each other ... and then slowly flowing back out again. The ocean itself is a very beautiful shade of blue ... a shade of blue that is so relaxing just to look at. You look out over the surface of the ocean all the way to the horizon, and then follow the horizon as far as you can see, noticing how it bends slightly downward as it follows the curvature of the earth. As you scan the ocean you can see, many miles offshore, a tiny sailboat skimming along the surface of the water. And all these sights help you to just let go and relax even more. As you continue walking down the beach, you become aware of the fresh, salty smell of the sea air. You take in a deep breath ... breathe out ... and feel very refreshed and even more relaxed. Overhead you notice two seagulls flying out to sea ... looking very graceful as they soar into the wind ... and you imagine how you might feel yourself if you had the freedom to fly. You find yourself settling into a deep state of relaxation as you continue walking down the beach. You feel the sea breeze blowing gently against your cheek and the warmth of the sun overhead penetrating your neck and shoulders. The warm, liquid sensation of the sun just relaxes you even more ... and you're beginning to feel perfectly content on this beautiful beach. It's such a lovely day. In a moment, up ahead, you see a comfortable-looking beach chair. Slowly, you begin to approach the beach chair ... and when you finally reach it, you sit back and settle in. Lying back in this comfortable beach chair, you let go and relax even more, drifting even deeper into relaxation. In a little while you might close your eyes and just listen to the sound of the surf, the unending cycle of waves ebbing and flowing. And the rhythmic sound of the surf carries you even deeper ... deeper still ... into a wonderful state of quietness and peace.

Exercise: A Guided Visualization of the Forest

You're walking along a path deep in the forest. All around you there are tall trees ... pine, fir, redwood, oak ... try to see them. The rushing sound of the wind blowing through the treetops is so soothing, allowing you to let go. You can smell the rich dampness of the forest floor, the smell of earth, and new seedlings, and rotting leaves. Now you look up through the treetops until you can see a light blue sky. You notice how high the sun is in the sky. As the sun enters the canopy of the treetops, it splinters into rays that penetrate through the trees to the forest floor. You're watching the intricate patterns of

*light and dark created as the light filters down
through the trees. The forest feels like a great
primeval cathedral ... filling you with a sense of
peace and reverence for all living things. Off in the
distance, you can hear the sound of rushing water
echoing through the forest. It gets louder as you
approach, and before long you are at the edge of a
mountain stream. You're looking at the stream,
noticing how clear and sparkling the water is.
Imagine sitting down and making yourself very
comfortable. You might sit down on a flat rock up
against a tree or you might even decide to lie down
on a grassy slope. You can see the mountain stream
creating rapids as it moves, rushing around a variety
of large and small rocks. These rocks are many
shades of brown, gray, and white and some are
covered with moss. You can see the sparkling water
rushing over some and around others, making
whirlpools and eddies. The rushing sound of the
water is so peaceful that you can just let yourself
drift ... relaxing more and more. You take in a deep
breath of fresh air and breathe out, finding the subtle
smells of the forest very refreshing. As you let
yourself sink into the soft bed of grass or dead leaves
or fragrant pine needles beneath you, let go of any
strains or concerns ... allowing the sights, sounds,
and smells of this beautiful forest to fill you with a
deep sense of peace.*

Practice Meditation

For most of us it is difficult to disentangle from our thoughts and simply experience ourselves in the present moment. Even when we withdraw our senses and are falling asleep at night, we usually experience a pastiche of memories, fantasies, thoughts, and feelings related to the preceding or coming day. Meditation is the one process that allows you to completely stop, let go of thoughts about the immediate past or future, and simply focus on being in the here and now. It also yields demonstrable relaxation effects. In 1968, Dr. Herbert Benson and his colleagues at Harvard Medical School measured the physiological reactions of a group of practitioners of transcendental meditation (Benson 1974). They found that:

- Heartbeat and breathing rates slowed

- Oxygen consumption fell by 20 percent

- Blood lactate levels (these rise with stress and fatigue) dropped

- Skin resistance to electrical current, a sign of relaxation, increased fourfold

- EEG measures of brain wave patterns indicated increased alpha activity, another sign of relaxation

Meditation practices have been around for at least 5,000 years. Traditionally, the purposes and benefits of meditation have been spiritual in nature: becoming one with God, attaining enlightenment, achieving selflessness. While many people still practice meditation today for spiritual purposes, just as many practice meditation apart from any religious framework, both for personal growth and for the simple purpose of relaxing.

Guidelines for Practicing Meditation

Find a quiet environment. Do what you can to reduce external noise. If this is not possible, play a CD or tape of soft instrumental sounds, or sounds from nature. The sound of ocean waves makes a good background.

Reduce muscle tension. If you're feeling tense, spend some time relaxing your muscles. Progressive muscle relaxation of your head, neck, and shoulders is often helpful (see chapter 1). The following sequence of head and neck exercises may also be helpful. You shouldn't spend more than ten minutes on this. First, slowly touch your chin to your chest three times, then bend your head back to gently stretch the back of your neck three times. Next bend your head over to your right shoulder three times, then bend your head over to your left shoulder three times, then slowly rotate your head clockwise for three complete rotations. Finally, slowly rotate your head counterclockwise for three complete rotations.

Sit properly. Sit in either of the following two positions. *Eastern Style:* Sit cross-legged on the floor with a cushion or pillow supporting your buttocks. Rest your hands on your thighs. Lean slightly forward so that some of your weight is supported by your thighs as well as your buttocks. *Western Style (preferred by most Americans):* Sit in a comfortable, straight-backed chair, with your feet on the floor and legs uncrossed, hands on your thighs.

In either position, keep your back and neck straight without straining to do so. Do not assume a tight, inflexible posture. If you need to scratch or move, do so. In general, do not lie down or support your head, as this will tend to promote sleep.

Make it a regular practice to meditate every day. Even if you meditate for only five minutes, it's important to do it every day. It's ideal if you can find a set time to practice meditating. Shortly we will show you two different meditations. Whichever you adopt, you might want to start out with short periods of five to ten minutes daily and gradually lengthen them to twenty to thirty minutes over a period of two to three weeks. You may wish to set a timer (within reach) or run a background tape that is twenty to thirty minutes long so that you'll know when you're done. If you prefer, use a clock or watch. After you have practiced twenty to thirty minutes per day for several weeks, you may wish to try longer periods of meditation up to an hour.

Don't meditate on a full stomach or when you are tired.

Select a focus for your attention. The most common devices are your own breathing cycle or a mantra (which we'll explain). Alternatives include a physical object, such as a picture or candle flame.

Assume a nonjudgmental, passive attitude. Concentrate on whatever you've chosen as an object of meditation but don't force or strain yourself to do so. If it is an internal mantra or image, you may want to close your eyes. When distracting thoughts or daydreams emerge, attempt neither to hold on to them nor to reject them too vigorously. Just allow them to come and go. Then bring your attention back to your object of focus. This process might be compared to watching leaves float by on the surface of a stream. Every time your attention wanders from your object of focus, gently bring it back again. Don't judge yourself when distractions come up.

Don't dwell on the outcome of your meditation. Let go of doubts such as whether you will be able to go deep enough in the remaining time. Refrain from judging your experience. There's no need to wonder how well you're doing during the meditation. Some meditations will feel good, some mediocre, and sometimes it may be difficult to meditate at all.

Let go. Refrain from trying to do anything other than gently guiding your attention back to your object of focus. The more you let go the deeper your meditation will be.

Exercise: Meditate Using a Mantra

---

1. Select a word to focus on. It can be an English word such as "calm," "peace," or "one," or a Sanskrit mantra such as "Om Shanti," "Sri Ram," or "Om Nameh Shivaya." "Now" is also a good choice because it tends to bring your focus into the present moment when said repeatedly. It can also be a word or phrase that has some special significance within your personal belief

system. In his book *Beyond the Relaxation Response,* Dr. Benson (1984) describes how a word or phrase of special personal or spiritual significance (such as "I am at peace" or "I abide in God") deepens the effects of meditation.

2. Repeat this word or phrase throughout your period of meditation, ideally on each exhalation.

3. As any thoughts come to mind, just let them pass over and through you. Then gently bring your attention back to the repetitive word or phrase.

Exercise: Counting Breaths

1. As you sit quietly, focus on the inflow and outflow of your breath. Each time you breathe out, count the breath. You can count up to ten or higher and start over again, or you can simply repeat the word "one" on each exhalation. Alternatively, you may prefer to start at ten or twenty and count backward on each exhalation down to zero, then start over.

2. Each time your focus wanders, bring it back to your breathing and counting. If you get caught in an internal monologue or fantasy, don't worry about it or judge yourself. Just relax and return to the count again.

3. If you lose track of the count, start over at one or at a round number like fifty or one hundred.

4. After practicing breath-counting meditation for a while, you may want to let go of the counting and just focus on the inflow and outflow of your breathing. The purpose of the counting is only to aid your concentration.

Stay the Course

Most people find that it takes persistent and disciplined effort over a period of several months to become proficient at meditating. Even though meditation is the most demanding of relaxation techniques, it is, for many people, the most rewarding. Research has found that among all relaxation techniques, meditation is the one people are most likely to persist in doing regularly.

Try Calming Music

Music has often been called the language of the soul. It seems to touch something deep within us. It can move you into inner spaces beyond your anxiety and worries. Relaxing music can help you to settle down into a place of serenity deep within that is impervious to the stresses and problems of daily life. It may also uplift you from a depressed mood. Whether you use music while driving, as a background while at work, or in the foreground when you want to take time out to relax, it is one of the most powerful and time-honored methods for letting go of anxiety or worry. If you use music to assuage anxiety, be sure to select pieces that are genuinely relaxing rather than stimulating or emotionally evocative.

If you're not near a tape or CD player, rely on a portable Walkman. The latter is particularly handy at night if you don't want to disturb others around you. You may find music to be a helpful background to relaxation techniques, such as progressive muscle relaxation or guided visualizations.

See the Resources section for a list of relaxing music selections.

Think Realistically

3

By the end of this chapter ...
  You will know how to:

- Recognize patterns of distorted thinking that spark anxiety

- Replace them with more realistic thoughts

What You Think Is What You Get

Imagine two individuals sitting in stop-and-go traffic at rush hour. One perceives himself as trapped, and says such things to himself as "I can't stand this," "I've got to get out of here," and "Why did I ever get myself into this commute?" What he feels is anxiety, anger, and frustration. The other perceives the situation as an opportunity to sit back, relax, and put on a new audiotape. He says such things to himself as "I might as well just relax and adjust to the pace of the traffic," or "I can unwind by doing some abdominal breathing and listening to the music." What he feels is a sense of calm and acceptance. In both cases, the situation is exactly the same, but the feelings in response to that situation are vastly different because of each individual's internal monologue, or self-talk.

The truth is that *it's what we say to ourselves in response to any particular situation that mainly determines our mood and feelings.* Often we say it so quickly and automatically that we don't even notice, and so we get the impression that the external situation "makes" us feel the way we do. But it's really our interpretations and thoughts about what is happening that form the basis of our feelings.

In short, you are largely responsible for how you feel (barring physiological determinants, such as illness). This is a profound and very important truth—one that sometimes takes a long time to fully grasp. It's often much easier to blame the way you feel on something or someone outside yourself than to take responsibility for your reactions. Yet it is through your willingness to accept that responsibility that you begin to take charge and have mastery over your life. The realization that you are mostly responsible for how you feel is empowering once you fully accept it. It's one of the most important keys to living a happier, more effective, and anxiety-free life.

People who suffer from anxiety are especially prone to engage in fearful self-talk. Anxiety can be generated on the spur of the moment by repeatedly making statements to yourself that begin with the two words: "what if." Any anxiety you experience in anticipation of confronting a difficult situation is manufactured out of your own what-if statements to yourself. When you decide to avoid a situation altogether, it is probably because of the scary questions you've asked yourself: "What if I panic?" "What if I can't handle it?" "What will other people think if they see me anxious?" Just noticing when you fall into what-if thinking is the first step toward gaining control over it. The real change occurs when you begin to counter and replace negative, what-if thoughts with positive, self-supportive statements that reinforce your ability to cope. For example, you might say, "So what," "These are just thoughts," "This is just scare-talk," or "I can handle this."

Catastrophizing

Fearful thinking takes many forms, but anxiety sufferers are often intimately acquainted with *catastrophizing*. We'll cover other varieties of distorted thinking later, but for now we'll focus on this most anxiety-producing pattern of thought. When you catastrophize, you imagine that some disaster is imminent. You predict dire consequences from unremarkable occurrences: a small leak in the sailboat means it will surely sink, feeling tired and fatigued often means that you have cancer, a slight downturn in the economy means you'll soon be jobless and out on the street.

Like all anxious thoughts, catastrophic thoughts usually start with the words "what if." "What if I break my leg skiing?" "What if my plane is hijacked?" "What if my son starts taking drugs?" "What if I'm in a car wreck?" "What if I flunk the exam and have to drop out of school?" "What if they see me panic and think I'm crazy?" There are no limits to a really fertile catastrophic imagination.

Overestimation and Underestimation

Catastrophizing relies on an *overestimation* of the odds of a bad outcome as well as an *underestimation* of your ability to cope with it should it befall you. What are the odds, *really*, that your fatigue is caused by cancer? What *really* is the likelihood that your son is taking drugs or that you'll break your leg skiing? And suppose the worst did happen. Would you *really* be unable to cope? People survive difficult, even dire situations all the time. Many of us know someone who's overcome a bout with cancer or trouble with a child. Certainly, these experiences would be difficult, undesirable, and trying, but what are the odds *really* that you could not weather them? If you take any fear and examine the thinking that fuels it, you'll often find catastrophizing at work. To the extent that you can overcome this distortion with more reality-based thinking, your anxiety will tend to drop away. In essence, you can define catastrophizing as *the unreasonable overestimation of some threat, coupled with an underestimation of your ability to cope with it.*

Challenge Catastrophizing

The following three steps are essential for challenging catastrophizing and undermining its power over you:

1. Identify the distorted thoughts.

2. Question their validity.

3. Replace them with more realistic thoughts.

Some examples of this follow.

Example #1: Fear of Serious Illness

Catastrophic pattern of thought. I have no energy and feel tired all the time. What if I have cancer and don't know it? If I were diagnosed with cancer, that would be the end. I couldn't take it. I'd be better off ending things quickly and killing myself.

Identify the distorted thoughts. The distorted thoughts are "Because I have low energy and feel tired, I must have cancer" and "If I had cancer, I certainly couldn't cope." In identifying distorted thoughts, first list all of your what-ifs about the situation, then change them to affirmative statements. For example, "What if my low energy and fatigue are signs of cancer?" would get changed to "Because I have low energy and fatigue, I have cancer."

Question their validity. What are the odds that low energy and fatigue mean that I have cancer? If the unlikely happened and I really was diagnosed with cancer, how terrible could that be? Would I actually go to pieces and not be able to continue living? Realistically, is it true that I would have no way of coping with the situation? Note how the questions begin. In challenging the validity of your catastrophic thoughts, it's helpful to use questions like: "What are the odds?" "Realistically, how likely is that?" "How often has that happened in the past?" or "If the worst did happen, is it really true that I'd not find *any* way to cope?"

Replace them with more realistic ones. Symptoms of fatigue and low energy can be indicative of all kinds of physical and psychological conditions, including a low-grade virus, anemia, adrenal exhaustion or hypothyroidism, depression, and food allergies, just to name a few. There are many possible explanations for my condition, and I don't have any specific symptoms that would indicate cancer. So the odds of my fatigue and low energy indicating cancer are very low. Moreover, bad as a cancer diagnosis would be, it's unlikely that I would totally go to pieces. After an initial difficult adjustment to the fact, which might take days to weeks, I would begin to think about what I needed to do to deal with the situation. It would certainly be difficult, but I wouldn't be less equipped to handle it than anyone else. My doctor and I would plan the most effective possible treatment strategies. I would join a local cancer support group, and draw lots of support from my friends and immediate family. I would supplement my treatment with alternative methods, such as visualization and dietary changes, which could aid recovery. In short, I would do everything possible to heal the condition.

Example #2: Fear of Panicking while Speaking before an Audience

Catastrophic pattern of thought. What if I start to panic while giving a talk to those people? What if they think I'm crazy? I'd never live it down.

Identify the distorted thoughts. The distorted thoughts are "I would surely panic if I had to give a talk" and "Others would definitely think I was crazy, which would be devastating to me."

Question their validity. Realistically, how likely is it that I would panic while speaking? What are the odds, if I did panic, that people would be aware of what I was thinking and thus conclude that I was crazy? Suppose the unlikely happened and people really thought I was crazy because I panicked. How terrible would that be? Is it realistic to suppose I'd never live it down?

Replace them with more realistic ones. If I did start to panic, I could simply abbreviate what I wanted to say and sit back down. As people tend to be caught up in their own thoughts and preoccupations, no one would likely notice my difficulty or be upset that I'd cut my comments short. Even if people did detect signs of panic, like my face turning red or my voice trembling, the odds are very slim that they'd think I was crazy or weird. Would I think that of someone if the roles were reversed? It's much more likely that they'd express concern. And even in the rare instance that someone thought I was crazy or different because I panicked, I could explain to them that I sometimes have a fear of speaking in public. With all the publicity about anxiety disorders these days, they would likely understand. Being totally honest is one way I could handle the situation. And no matter what happened, I would forget about it after a while. It's just not true that I would never live it down. I've gotten over embarrassment before.

Example #3: Fear of Losing Your Job

Catastrophic pattern of thought. The economy has tightened in the last couple of years and layoffs are skyrocketing. What if I lose my job and can't pay my rent? I'll be out on the street and never be able to get back on my feet again. I'd be too embarrassed to ask my family and friends for help. I'd be at the mercy of strangers.

Identify the distorted thoughts. The distorted thoughts are "A faltering economy will result in the loss of my job" and "Losing my job would leave me destitute and helpless."

Question their validity. How likely am I really to lose my job? Suppose I did. Would I really wind up homeless? Would I really have no way of picking myself up? Would it really be impossible to ask for help from family and friends?

Replace them with more realistic ones. My company is showing no signs of real financial distress, and even if I did lose my job, I'd have ways of coping. Most people are still working, and I could find another job. I'm hardworking and good at what I do. I have supportive family members and friends whom I've helped in the past. If I couldn't pay my rent, I could stay with them until I got back on my feet. I have a little savings and, if worst came to worst, I could cash in my 401(k) plan. Also, I could receive unemployment for a while if I were laid off. It would be difficult, but not insurmountable.

The above three examples illustrate how fear-producing catastrophic thoughts can be challenged and countered by more realistic, less anxious thinking. Now it's your turn. After the guidelines below, you will find the Realistic Thoughts Worksheet. Before you begin this exercise, make at least twenty copies of the worksheet, since you will use it many times (you can photocopy the page in the book or simply type and print out the five parts of the worksheet on your computer). Once you've made copies of the worksheet, follow the guidelines below to counter fearful thoughts associated with any fearful situation or worry.

Guidelines for Challenging Fearful Thoughts

1. Pick a time when you're relatively relaxed and calm, preferably not in the middle of an episode of intense anxiety or worry. Find a way to relax and center yourself first (see chapters 1 and 2) before you work on countering your fearful thoughts.

2. After you get somewhat relaxed, ask yourself: "What was I telling myself that made me anxious?" Think of

all the what-if thoughts you were telling yourself and write them under the first subhead on the worksheet: What I Was Telling Myself.

3. To make your distorted thoughts more clear and easy to challenge, change them from what-if statements to regular, affirmative statements. It is easier to see the distortion when you change a what-if thought like "What if this plane crashes" to the definite statement: "This plane is going to crash." Write your revised thoughts under the second subhead on the worksheet: Distorted Patterns of Thought.

4. Challenge your distorted thoughts by asking questions such as "What are the realistic odds of this happening?" "How often has this happened in the past?" "Am I viewing this situation as completely unmanageable or unsurvivable?"

5. Use the questions to come up with more realistic thoughts about the situation or worry. Write these realistic thoughts under the subhead: More Realistic Thought Patterns.

6. Finally, think about ways you could cope if your worst fear happened. Ask yourself, "If the worst happened, what could I do to cope?" In most cases, this will help you to see that you underestimated your ability to cope. Write your ways of coping under the subhead: If the Worst Did Happen, What I Could Do to Cope.

7. Reread the realistic thoughts and ways you could cope with the worst-case scenario many times over a few weeks. This will reinforce them strongly in your mind. You might want to rewrite these statements on an index card that you keep with you and can pull out at a moment's notice.

8. Repeat all of the steps of this exercise, using a separate copy of the worksheet, for each of your fears or worries.

Realistic Thoughts Worksheet

What I Was Telling Myself
    (List your what-ifs about the feared situation.)

Distorted Patterns of Thought
    (Turn your what-ifs into regular statements. For example, "What if I panic?" would change to "I'm going to panic." "What if they think I'm stupid?" changes to "They will think I'm stupid.")

Challenge Your Distortions
    (Ask questions such as "What are the realistic odds of this happening?" "How often has this happened in the past?" "Am I viewing this situation as completely unmanageable or unsurvivable?")

More Realistic Thought Patterns
    (Replace your distorted, fearful patterns of thought with more realistic thoughts about the situation.)

If the Worst Did Happen, What I Could Do to Cope
    (List ways you would cope if your imagined worst-case scenario, however unlikely, actually came true.)

Other Distorted Patterns of Thought

Catastrophizing is not the only pattern of distorted thinking that can trigger anxiety. Here we'll discuss seven others. You many recognize many or all of them.

Filtering

You focus on the negative details while ignoring all the positive aspects of a situation. For example, a computer draftsman who was uncomfortable with criticism was praised for the quality of his recent detail drawings and was asked if he could get the next job out a little more quickly. He went home anxious, having decided that his employer thought he was dawdling. He filtered out the praise and focused only on the criticism.

Polarized Thinking

Things are black or white, good or bad. You have to be perfect or you're a failure. There's no middle ground, no room for mistakes. A single mother with three children was determined to be strong and "in charge." The moment she felt tired or confused, she began thinking of herself as a bad mother and became anxious.

Overgeneralization

You reach a general conclusion based on a single incident or piece of evidence. You exaggerate the frequency of problems and use negative global labels. This pattern can lead to an increasingly restricted life. If you got sick on a train once, you decide never to take a train again. If you got dizzy on a sixth-floor balcony, you never go out there again. If you felt anxious the last time your husband took a business trip, you imagine you'll be a wreck every time he leaves town. One bad experience means that whenever you're in a similar situation you will inevitably repeat the bad experience. It's easy to see how this could contribute to anxiety. Words such as "always" or "never" are clues to overgeneralized thinking.

Mind Reading

Without their saying so, you just "know" what people are feeling and why they act the way they do. In particular, you have certain knowledge of how people think and feel about you. You're afraid to actually check it out with them. You might assume what your boyfriend is thinking and say to yourself, "This close he sees how unattractive I am." You then become anxious because you think he's going to reject you.

Magnifying

You exaggerate the degree or intensity of a problem. You turn up the volume on anything bad, making it loud, large, and overwhelming. Minor suggestions become scathing criticism. Minor setbacks become cause for despair. Slight obstacles become overwhelming barriers. The flip side of magnifying is minimizing. When you magnify, you view everything negative and difficult in your life through a telescope that magnifies your problems. But when you view your assets, such as your ability to cope and find solutions, you look through the wrong end of the telescope so that everything positive is minimized. This pattern creates a tone of doom and hysterical pessimism, which easily gives way to anxiety.

Personalization

You assume that everything people do or say is some kind of reaction to you. You also frequently compare yourself to others, trying to determine who is smarter, more competent, better looking, and so on. Because of this, you view your own worth as dependent on how you measure up to others. And you become anxious, worrying about whether you measure up.

Shoulds

You have a list of ironclad rules about how you and other people should act. People who break the rules anger you, and you feel guilty when you violate the rules. "I should be the *perfect* friend, parent, teacher, student, or spouse"; "I should know, understand, and foresee everything"; "I should be nice and never display anger"; and "I should never make mistakes" are examples of unrealistic "shoulds." Your personal code of conduct is so demanding that it's impossible to live up to and you make yourself anxious just thinking about it.

Exercise: Recognizing the Patterns

The following exercise is designed to help you notice and identify distorted thinking patterns. Read each statement carefully and refer back to the above summary to see how each statement or situation is based on one or more forms of distorted thinking.

1. The washing machine breaks down. A mother with twins in diapers says to herself, "This always happens. I can't stand it. The whole day's ruined."

2. "He looked up from across the table and said, 'That's interesting.' I knew he was dying for breakfast to be over so he could get away from me."

3. A man was trying to get his girlfriend to be warmer and more supportive. He got irritated every night when she didn't ask him how his day was or failed to give him the attention he expected.

4. A driver feels nervous on long trips, afraid of having car trouble or getting sick and being stranded far from home. Faced with having to drive 500 miles to Chicago and back, he tells himself, "It's too far. My car has over 60,000 miles on it—it'll never make it."

5. Getting ready for the prom, a high school student thinks, "I've got the worst hips in my homeroom, and the second-worst hair ... If this French twist comes undone, I'll just die. I'll never get it back together and the evening will be ruined ... I hope Ron gets his dad's car. If only he does, everything will be perfect."

Answers 1. Overgeneralization, Filtering; 2. Mind Reading; 3. Shoulds; 4. Catastrophizing, Magnifying; 5. Personalization, Polarized Thinking, Catastrophizing.

Seven Solutions for Seven Distortions

Below are some useful methods for balancing the distorted patterns of thought that spark anxiety.

Filtering

You have been stuck in a mental groove, focusing on things from your environment that frighten you. In order to conquer filtering you will have to deliberately shift focus. You can shift focus in two ways. First, focus on the solution instead of the problem. Place your attention on coping strategies for dealing with the problem, rather than obsessing about the problem itself. Second, focus on the opposite of your primary mental theme, which, with anxiety, is danger or insecurity. Focus instead on things in your environment that represent comfort and safety. A classic question to ask with all forms of filtering is: "Am I seeing the glass half empty or half full?"

Polarized Thinking

The key to overcoming polarized thinking is to stop making black-or-white judgments. Think in terms of percentages: "About 30 percent of me is scared to death, and 70 percent is holding on and coping."

Overgeneralization

Overgeneralization is exaggeration—the tendency to take a button and sew a vest on it. Fight it by *quantifying* instead of using words like *huge, awful, massive, minuscule,* and so on. For example, if you catch yourself thinking, "We're buried under massive debt," rephrase with a quantity: "We owe $27,000."

Mind Reading

In the long run, you are probably better off making no inferences at all about people's internal thoughts. Either believe what they tell you or hold no belief at all until some conclusive evidence comes your way. Treat all of your notions about people as hypotheses to be tested and checked out by asking them. Sometimes you can't check out your interpretations. For instance, you may not be ready to ask your daughter if her withdrawal from family life means she's pregnant or taking drugs. But you can allay your anxiety by generating alternative interpretations of her behavior. Perhaps she's in love. Or premenstrual. Or studying hard. Or depressed about something. By generating a string of possibilities, you may find a more neutral interpretation that is more likely to be true than your direst suspicions.

Magnifying

To combat magnifying, stop using words like *terrible, awful, disgusting,* or *horrendous.* In particular, banish phrases like "I can't stand it," "It's impossible," or "It's unbearable." You can stand it, because history shows that human beings can survive almost any psychological blow and can endure incredible physical pain. You can get used to and cope with almost anything. Try saying to yourself phrases such as "I can cope" and "I can survive this."

Personalization

When you catch yourself comparing yourself to others, remind yourself that everyone has strong and weak points. By matching your weak points to other people's corresponding strong points, you are just looking for ways to demoralize yourself. If you assume that the reactions of others are often about you, force yourself to check it out. Maybe the boss *isn't* frowning because you're late. Draw no conclusions unless you are satisfied that you have reasonable evidence and proof.

Shoulds

Reexamine and question any personal rules or expectations that include the words *should, ought, have to,* or *must.* Flexible rules and expectations don't use these words because there are always exceptions and special circumstances. Think of at least three exceptions to your rule, and then imagine all the exceptions there must be that you can't think of. You can soften shoulds, have-tos, and musts by replacing them with the notion "prefer." You don't *have to* win the competition or look perfect, you'd just prefer to.

Face Your Fears

4

By the end of this chapter ...
  You will know how to:

- Use exposure therapy to confront phobic situations in real life and overcome your fear

- Use systematic desensitization to mentally face those phobic situations that cannot be confronted in real life and overcome your fear

Let's Face It

The most effective way to overcome a phobia is simply to face it. Continuing to avoid a phobic situation only feeds the fear you're trying so hard to banish. To someone struggling with phobia-related anxiety, this can seem like a stark declaration. In fact, if you just thought *No way!* we're not surprised. At the outset, even the thought of facing a situation you've avoided for a long time seems daunting at best and downright impossible at worst. But exposure is a gradual, step-by-step process, *not* a sudden immersion. You'll face your fears in small, even minute, increments. This is part and parcel of "exposure therapy," which involves a comprehensive plan to face your phobias in real life when feasible or in imagination when not.

Phobia-Related Anxiety

For many people anxiety stems from phobias. A phobia is an exaggerated fear of a particular situation or experience that causes your anxiety to spike. Usually, you avoid the situation. In some cases even the thought of the feared situation is enough to trigger your anxiety. The fear and avoidance are strong enough to interfere with your normal routines, work, or relationships, and to cause you significant distress. Common phobias include fear of riding in elevators, fear of public speaking, fear of flying, fear of visiting the doctor or dentist, and fear of heights. If you have a phobia, your anxiety does not come out of the blue, as it does for some people. It is caused by the thought or the real possibility of being in a feared situation.

Sensitization

Phobias are developed by *sensitization*. This is a process of becoming sensitized to a particular stimulus. In the case of phobias, it involves learning to associate anxiety with a particular situation. Perhaps you once panicked while riding in an elevator or giving a talk. If your anxiety level was high, it's likely that you acquired a strong association between being in that particular situation and being anxious. Thereafter, being in, near, or perhaps just thinking about the situation automatically triggered your anxiety. A connection between the situation and a strong anxiety response was established. Because this connection was automatic and seemingly beyond your control, you probably did all you could to avoid putting yourself in the situation again. Your avoidance was rewarded because it saved you from reexperiencing your anxiety. At the point where you began to always avoid the situation, you developed a full-fledged phobia.

Exposure Therapy

Exposure therapy (also called *real-life desensitization, in vivo desensitization, exposure treatment,* or simply *exposure*) is a process of *desensitizing* yourself to your phobia. With exposure, you confront a phobic situation by completing a series of activities, called a *hierarchy,* that brings you progressively, but ultimately, into the situation you fear. *Desensitization* is the goal. Exposure therapy involves:

1. *unlearning* the connection between a phobic situation (such as public speaking) and an anxiety response, and

2. *reassociating* feelings of relaxation and calmness with that particular situation.

A phobia hinges upon a particular situation being invested with an unrealistic and unsettling danger. When you desensitize to the phobic situation, it is normalized. It just ceases to have the power to emotionally unseat you.

Creating a Hierarchy

Exposure therapy works by creating a hierarchy. This is a series of steps that bring you incrementally closer to being in your feared situation. You can think of it as a graduated scale, with the first step being, at most, mildly anxiety producing and the last being strongly anxiety producing. Generally, eight to twelve steps in a hierarchy are sufficient, although in some cases you may want to include as many as twenty. Fewer than eight steps is usually not enough to make the hierarchy effective. Sometimes you may find it difficult to go from one step to the next. You may be able to negotiate step 9, but become very anxious when you face step 10. In this instance you need to construct an intermediate step (9½) that can serve as a bridge between the two original steps. You may want to have a support person accompany you when you first face your phobia or on those steps that arouse more anxiety.

Example: A Hierarchy for Overcoming Elevator Phobia

1. Look at elevators, watching them come and go.
2. Stand in a stationary elevator with your support person.
3. Stand in a stationary elevator alone.
4. Travel up or down one floor with your support person.
5. Travel up or down one floor alone, with your support person waiting outside the elevator on the floor where you will arrive.
6. Travel two to three floors with your support person.
7. Travel two to three floors alone, with your support person waiting outside the elevator on the floor where you will arrive.
8. Extend the number of floors you travel, first with your support person and then alone with your support person waiting outside the elevator.
9. Travel on an elevator alone without your support person.

See the Resources section at the end of this book for additional examples of hierarchies.

Knowing When to Retreat

When you begin acting out the steps of a hierarchy, there may be times when you have to temporarily retreat because your anxiety reaches a certain level. Use the Anxiety Scale below as a barometer of your anxiety's intensity. Although it may not correspond exactly to your specific symptoms, the scale outlines typical symptoms at various intensity levels. The important thing is to identify what constitutes level 4 for *you*. This is the point at which, whatever symptoms you're experiencing, you feel your control over your reaction beginning to diminish—and it is the time to retreat.

Anxiety Scale

7–10 *Major Panic Attack*
All of the symptoms in level 6 exaggerated, terror, fear of going crazy or dying, strong compulsion to escape

6 *Moderate Panic Attack*
Palpitations, difficulty breathing, feeling disoriented or detached (feeling of unreality), panic in response to perceived loss of control

5 *Early Panic*
Heart pounding or beating irregularly, constricted breathing, spaciness or dizziness, definite fear of losing control, compulsion to escape

4 *Marked Anxiety*
Feeling uncomfortable or spacey, heart beating fast, muscles tight, beginning to wonder about maintaining control

3 *Moderate Anxiety*
Feeling uncomfortable but still in control, heart starting to beat faster, more rapid breathing, sweaty palms

2 *Mild Anxiety*
Butterflies in stomach, muscle tension, definitely nervous

1 *Slight Anxiety*
Passing twinge of anxiety, feeling slightly nervous

0 *Relaxation*
Calm, a feeling of being undistracted and at peace

Optional: Try Imagery Desensitization First

Some people like to practice a technique called *imagery desensitization* before navigating a phobic situation in real life. This involves visualizing the experiences outlined in your hierarchy rather than confronting them in real life. If you wish to use this as a precursor to real-life exposure see "Imagery Desensitization" later in this chapter.

How to Do Exposure

To design your exposure therapy, start out by clearly defining your goals. What would constitute being fully recovered from your phobias? Do you want to be able to drive on the freeway alone? Buy the week's groceries by yourself? Give a presentation at work? Fly on a jet? Be sure to make your goals specific. Instead of aiming for something as broad as being comfortable shopping, define a specific goal such as buying three items in the grocery store by yourself. For the purpose of creating a hierarchy, keep your goals concrete.

You're ready now to break each goal down into small, incremental steps. On a sheet of paper, list the steps of your hierarchy. If necessary, refer back to the elevator phobia example earlier in this chapter. Be sure to start off with a simple, only mildly anxiety-arousing step and work up to a final step that you would be able to do if you were fully recovered from your phobia. Your hierarchy should have from eight to twenty progressively more difficult steps. Start with a relatively easy or mild instance of facing your fearful situation. Develop at least eight steps that involve progressively more challenging exposures. The final step should be your goal or even a step beyond what you've designated as your goal. Next to each step in the hierarchy, note the date you complete it. When you've completed your hierarchy for your first goal (for example, flying), write another hierarchy for your next goal (for example, elevators), and so on.

Basic Procedure for Exposure

Proceed into your phobic situation, beginning with the first step on your hierarchy or the one at which you last left off. Continue to proceed up the steps of your hierarchy until the point where your anxiety first begins to feel unmanageable (level 4 on the anxiety scale). If it doesn't feel unmanageable, great. *Just stay in your fearful situation until your anxiety begins to* *subside.* Even if you are uncomfortable in the situation, stay with it as long as your anxiety level does not go to the point where it begins to feel unmanageable. *Allow time to pass and let your anxiety diminish.* When undertaking exposure, it's very helpful to practice the abdominal breathing technique described in chapter 1. Breathing from your abdomen can help to diffuse some of the anxiety that comes up.

Retreat from the situation if you feel like your anxiety has reached a point where it might get out of control, that is, above level 4 on the Anxiety Scale. Retreating means temporarily leaving the situation until you feel better and then returning. In most situations this is literally possible, but when it is not—for example, when you are aboard an airplane—you can retreat to a peaceful scene in your mind. Retreat is not the same as escaping or avoiding the situation. It is designed to prevent resensitization to the situation.

Recover. Should you temporarily pull back from your phobic situation, wait until your anxiety level diminishes. Be sure to give yourself sufficient time for your anxiety to subside. You may find that abdominal breathing or walking around at this point helps you recover your equanimity.

Repeat. After recovering, reenter your phobic situation and continue to progress up through your hierarchy to the point where you feel either tired or you feel like your anxiety might get unmanageable. If you are able to go further or stay longer in the situation than you did before, fine. If not, or if you can't go even as far as you did the first time, that's fine too. Do not chastise yourself if your performance after retreating turns out to be less spectacular than it was initially. This is a common experience. In a day or two you'll find that you'll be able to continue in your progression up your hierarchy.

   Continue going through the above cycle—Expose-Retreat (if necessary)-Recover-Repeat—until you begin to feel tired or bored, then stop for the day. Progress through as many steps in your hierarchy as you feel able to. This constitutes one practice session, and it will typically take you from thirty minutes to two hours. For most people one practice session per day is enough. Be aware that your progress through the steps in your hierarchy is likely to be uneven. On some days you'll enjoy excellent progress, perhaps going through several steps. On others you may hardly progress at all, and on still others you will not go as far as you did on preceding days. On a given Monday you might spend five minutes alone in the grocery store for the first time in years. On Tuesday you can endure five minutes again but no more. Then on Wednesday you are unable to go into the store at all. Thursday or Friday, however, you discover that you can last ten minutes in the store. This up-and-down, two-steps-forward-one-step-back phenomenon is typical of exposure therapy. Don't let it discourage you!

Making the Most of Exposure Therapy

Following these guidelines will help you reap the most benefit from exposure therapy.

Rely on a Support Person

It's often very helpful to rely on a person you trust (such as your spouse, partner, friend, or a helping professional) to accompany you on your forays into your phobia hierarchy, especially when you first begin the process of exposure. The support person can provide reassurance and safety, distraction (by talking with you), encouragement to persist, and praise for your incremental successes. However, your support person shouldn't push you. It's up to you to determine the pace that you move up your hierarchy. It is helpful, though, if your support person can identify any resistance on your part and help you to recognize whether such resistance is present. Your partner's main job is to provide encouragement and support without judging your performance. As you progress through your hierarchy, you will eventually fly solo and face your fearful situation on your own.

Be Willing to Take Risks

Entering a phobic situation that you've been avoiding for a long time means taking a mild to moderate risk. Risk-taking is easier, however, when you construct your hierarchy with small, limited goals and proceed incrementally.

Cope with Resistance

Undertaking exposure to a situation that you've been avoiding may bring up resistance. Notice if you delay getting started with your exposure sessions or find reasons to procrastinate. The mere thought of actually entering a phobic situation may elicit strong anxiety, a fear of being trapped, or self-defeating statements to yourself such as "I'll never be able to do it" or "This is hopeless." Instead of getting stuck in resistance, try to regard the process of desensitization as a major therapeutic opportunity. Give yourself pep talks about how much your life and relationships will improve when you are no longer plagued by your phobias. Once you get through any initial resistance to real-life exposure, the going gets easier. If you feel you're having problems with resistance at any point, you may want to consult a therapist who is familiar with exposure therapy.

Be Willing to Tolerate Some Discomfort

It's inevitable that you will experience some anxiety in the course of becoming desensitized. Initially you many even feel worse. Recognize that feeling worse means you're laying the foundation to feel better. As you become more skilled at exposure, your practice sessions will become easier and you'll gain more confidence about following through to completion.

Avoid "Flooding" and Be Willing to Retreat

In the process of desensitization, you are in control of the intensity and length of your exposure to the situations that frighten you. Always be willing to retreat from a practice situation if your anxiety seems like it's becoming overwhelming (above level 4 on the Anxiety Scale). Then wait until you recover before confronting the phobic situation again. Flooding or overexposure may resensitize you to the phobic situation.

Plan for Contingencies

Suppose you're practicing on an elevator and the worst happens: it stops between floors. Or suppose you are just beginning to drive on the freeway and you start to panic when you're far away from an exit. It's wise to plan ahead for those worst-case scenarios whenever possible. In the first example, give yourself some insurance by practicing on an elevator that has a functioning emergency phone. Or in the case of the freeway, tell yourself in advance that it will be all right to retreat to the shoulder or at least drive slowly with your emergency flashers on until you reach an exit. If you'll be entering a situation that doesn't have an escape hatch, bring along a relaxation cassette and a tape player with headphones, or a cell phone.

Trust Your Own Pace

It's important not to regard exposure as some kind of race. The goal is not to see how fast you can overcome the problem. Pressuring yourself to make great strides quickly carries the risk of resensitizing yourself to your phobia.

Reward Yourself for Small Successes

Rewarding yourself for small successes will help sustain your motivation to keep practicing. For example, being able to go into a phobic situation slightly further than the day before is worthy of giving yourself a reward, such as a new piece of clothing or dinner out. So is being able to stay in the situation a few moments longer or being able to tolerate anxious feelings a few moments longer.

Learn to Cope with the Early Stages of Panic

Use your array of coping techniques that you learned in earlier chapters if you are unable to easily retreat from a situation. Remember to maintain an overall attitude of floating or going with your bodily sensations rather than balking at or resisting them. If you feel like you need to retreat, use this option!

Use Positive Coping Statements

Use any of the following coping statements before or during your exposure session:

This is an opportunity for me to learn to be comfortable with this situation.

Facing my fear of _____ is the best way to overcome my anxiety about it.

Each time I choose to face _____, I take another step toward becoming free of fear.

By taking this step now, I'm getting closer to doing what I want.

I know I'll feel better once I'm actually in the situation.

There is always a way to retreat from this situation if I need to.

I've handled this before and I can handle it now.

It's only my thinking that would make me feel trapped. I can change my thinking and feel free.

Nothing serious is going to happen to me.

This is not as bad as I've imagined.

As I continue to practice, this will get easier.

Any anxiety I feel is just a reminder to use my coping skills.

These feeling will pass and I'll be okay.

This is just adrenaline—it will pass.

These are just thoughts—not reality.

Nothing about this sensation or feeling is dangerous.

I can handle this.

You may want to write some of the above statements on an index card and carry it with you during your practice sessions.

Practice Regularly

Ideally, you should practice real-life desensitization three to five times per week. Longer practice sessions, with several trials of exposure to your phobic situation, tend to produce more rapid results than shorter sessions. As long as you retreat when appropriate, it's impossible to undergo too much exposure in a given practice session (the worst that can happen is that you might end up somewhat tired or drained). *Regular, frequent practice is the key to successful exposure.*

Expect and Know How to Handle Setbacks

Not being able to tolerate as much exposure to a situation as you did previously is a normal part of recovery. Recovery simply doesn't proceed in a linear fashion. There will be plateaus and regressions as well as times of moving forward. Setbacks are an integral part of the recovery process. Above all, don't let a setback discourage you from further practice. Simply chalk it up to a bad day or bad week and learn from it.

Be Prepared to Experience Stronger Emotions

Facing phobic situations you've been avoiding for a long time often stirs up suppressed feelings of not only anxiety but anger and sorrow as well. Recognize that this is a normal and expected part of the recovery process. Let yourself know it's okay to have these feelings even though you may be uncomfortable with them.

Follow Through to Completion

Finishing exposure therapy means that you reach a point where you are no longer afraid of anxiety in any situation that was formerly a problem. (Obviously this does not include extreme situations that anyone would fear.) The recovery process generally takes from a month to a year depending on how many phobias you address and how often you practice. Getting comfortable with most situations but still having one or two you are afraid of is generally insufficient. To attain lasting freedom from your phobias, it's important to keep working until you get to the point where you can go into any situation that nonphobic people would regard as safe, and you regard anxiety reactions themselves as manageable and not at all dangerous.

Put Aside Props and Crutches

In the early-to-middle stages of exposure, relying on props and crutches such as a support person, a tranquilizer, or "security devices" such as a lucky pendant or cell phone may be necessary and useful in helping you to reduce anxiety. If your goal is merely to be able to *cope* with facing difficult situations such as driving expressways, flying, or giving a talk, you may choose to continue to rely on such resources indefinitely. However, if your goal is to fully *overcome* your fear, then all such props and crutches eventually need to be relinquished.

Systematic (or Imagery) Desensitization

What if facing your fear in real life is impractical? For example, if you fear taking a transcontinental flight, repeated real-life exposure is not a practical option. Using a technique called systematic desensitization, you can help to unravel this kind of phobia. Like real-life exposure it relies on a hierarchy of progressively anxiety-inducing steps. The difference is that you *visualize* yourself undertaking them rather than acting them out in real life. Sometimes systematic desensitization is helpful to do in advance of facing a phobic situation through real-life exposure.

Guidelines for Systematic Desensitization

To design your imagery desensitization, choose a particular phobic situation you want to work on; for example, flying. Then create your hierarchy. Imagine having to deal with this situation in a very limited way—one that hardly bothers you at all. You can create this scenario by imagining yourself somewhat removed in space or time from full exposure to the situation, such as parking in front of the airport without going in, or imagining your feelings one month before you have to make a flight. Or you can diminish the difficulty of the situation by visualizing yourself with a supportive person at your side. Try in these ways to create a very mild instance of your phobia and designate it as the first step in your hierarchy.

Imagine what would be the strongest or most challenging scene relating to your phobia, and place it at the opposite extreme as the highest step in your hierarchy. For flying, such a step might involve taking off on a transcontinental flight, or encountering severe air turbulence midflight. Now take some time to imagine eight or more scenes of graduated intensity related to your phobia and rank them according to their anxiety-provoking potential. Intermediate scenes for flying might include the point of getting on the plane, the point where the flight attendant locks the door, the point of takeoff, and so on. If you are planning to eventually face the fear in real life it is desirable to have these scenes correspond to things you will actually do at that time. Place your scenes in ascending order between the two extremes you've already defined.

Basic Procedure for Systematic (Imagery) Desensitization

1. Spend a few minutes getting relaxed. Use progressive muscle relaxation or any other relaxation technique that works well for you.

2. Visualize yourself in a peaceful scene. This is a relaxing place you can vividly picture in your mind. It can be a scene outdoors (such as a beach, a meadow, or the mountains), indoors (curling up by a fireplace), or can come completely from your imagination. Above all it is a place where you feel safe. Spend about one minute there.

3. Visualize yourself in the first scene of your phobia hierarchy. Stay there for thirty seconds to one minute, trying to picture everything with as much vividness and detail as possible, as if you were right there. Imagine yourself acting and feeling calm and confident. If you feel little or no anxiety, proceed to the next scene up in your hierarchy.

4. On the other hand, if you experience mild to moderate anxiety, try to stay a full thirty seconds to one minute in the scene, allowing yourself to relax into it. You can do this by breathing away any anxious sensations in your body or by repeating a calming affirmation such as "I am calm and at ease." Picture yourself handling the situation in a calm and confident manner.

5. After up to a minute of exposure, retreat from the phobic scene to your peaceful scene. Spend about one minute in your peaceful scene or long enough to get fully

relaxed. Then repeat your visualization of the same phobic scene as in step 4 for thirty seconds to one minute. Keep alternating between a given phobic scene and your peaceful scene (about one minute each) until the phobic scene loses its capacity to elicit any (or more than minimal) anxiety. Then you are ready to proceed to the next step up in your hierarchy.

6. If visualizing a particular scene causes strong anxiety, especially if you feel you're approaching panic (see the Anxiety Scale earlier in this chapter), do not spend more than ten seconds there. Retreat immediately to your peaceful scene and stay there until you're fully relaxed. Expose yourself gradually to the more difficult scenes, alternating short intervals of exposure with retreat to your peaceful scene. If a particular scene in your hierarchy continues to cause difficulty, you probably need to add another step—one that is intermediate in difficulty between the last step you completed successfully and the one that is troublesome.

7. Continue progressing up your hierarchy step-by-step. Generally, it will take a minimum of two exposures to a scene to reduce your anxiety to it. Keep in mind that it's important not to go on to a more advanced step until you're fully comfortable with the preceding step. Practice systematic desensitization for fifteen to twenty minutes each day. Begin each practice session not with a new step but with the last step you successfully negotiated. Then go on to a new step.

Get Regular Exercise

By the end of this chapter ...
You will know how to:

- Maximize the anxiety-reducing effects of exercise
- Develop the exercise program that best meets your needs
- Counter common excuses for not exercising

You *Can* Run (or Swim, If You Prefer) from Your Fear

Regular, vigorous exercise is one of the most powerful and effective methods of reducing anxiety. When you experience anxiety, your body's natural fight-or-flight reaction—the sudden surge of adrenaline in response to a threat—becomes excessive. Exercise is a natural outlet for your body when it is in the fight-or-flight mode of arousal. Regular exercise also diminishes the tendency to experience anticipatory anxiety toward phobic situations, expediting recovery from all kinds of phobias.

Muscles Aren't the Only Thing Exercise Strengthens

Regular exercise has a direct impact on several physiological factors that underlie anxiety, and as a result it strengthens your defenses against anxiety. Some of these physiological benefits include:

- reduced skeletal muscle tension, which is largely responsible for your feelings of being tense or "uptight"

- more rapid metabolism of excess adrenaline and thyroxin in the bloodstream, the presence of which tends to keep you in a state of arousal and vigilance

- discharge of pent-up frustration, which can aggravate phobic reactions

- enhanced oxygenation of the blood and brain, which increases alertness and concentration

- stimulation of the production of *endorphins,* natural substances that resemble morphine in both their chemical makeup and their effect on your sense of well-being

- increased brain levels of serotonin (an important neurotransmitter), helping to offset both depressed moods and anxiety

- lowered pH (increased acidity) of the blood, which increases your energy level

- improved circulation

- improved digestion and utilization of food

- improved elimination (from skin, lungs, and bowels)

- decreased cholesterol levels

- decreased blood pressure

- weight loss as well as appetite suppression in many cases

- improved blood sugar regulation (in the case of hypoglycemia)

Several *psychological* benefits accompany these physical shifts, including:

- increased subjective feelings of well-being

- reduced dependence on alcohol and drugs

- reduced insomnia

- improved concentration and memory

- reduced depression

- increased self-esteem

- greater sense of control over anxiety

Are You Ready for an Exercise Program?

There are certain physical conditions that limit the amount and intensity of exercise you should undertake. Ask yourself the eight questions below before launching a program of regular exercise. If your answer to any of them is yes, be sure to consult your physician before beginning an exercise routine. He or she may recommend a program of restricted or supervised exercise appropriate to your needs.

1. Has your physician ever said you have heart trouble?

2. Do you frequently have pains in your heart or chest?

3. Do you often feel faint or have spells of dizziness?

4. Has your physician ever told you that you have a bone or joint problem (such as arthritis) that has been or might be aggravated by exercise?

5. Has a physician ever said that your blood pressure was too high?

6. Do you have diabetes?

7. Are you over forty years old and unaccustomed to vigorous exercise?

8. Is there a physical reason, not mentioned here, why you should not undertake an exercise program?

If you answered no to all of the above questions, you can be reasonably assured that you are ready to start an exercise program. Begin slowly and increase your activity gradually over a period of weeks. If you are over forty and unaccustomed to exercise, plan to see your doctor for a physical exam before undertaking an exercise program. It might also be helpful to have a support person exercise with you initially. If you feel phobic about exercise, a program of gradual exposure will help you to desensitize to it in the same way you would to any other phobia (see chapter 4).

Optimizing the Anxiety-Reducing Effects of Exercise

Exercise needs to be of sufficient regularity, intensity, and duration to have a significant impact on anxiety. Aim for the following standards:

• Ideally exercise should be *aerobic.*

• Optimal frequency is *four to five times* per week.

• Optimal duration is *twenty to thirty minutes* or more per session.

• Optimal intensity for aerobic exercise is a heart rate of *(220 − your age) x 0.75* for at least ten minutes.

Aerobic Pulse Ranges by Age

Age	Pulse (Heart) Rate
20–29	145–164
30–39	138–156
40–49	130–148
50–59	122–140
60–69	116–132

Avoid exercising only once per week. Engaging in infrequent spurts of exercise is stressful to your body and generally does more harm than good. (Walking is an exception.)

Exercise for Your Needs

Which forms of exercise you select depends upon your objectives. For reducing anxiety, aerobic exercise is typically the most effective. Aerobic exercise requires sustained activity of your larger muscles. It reduces skeletal muscle tension and increases cardiovascular conditioning—the capacity of your circulatory system to deliver oxygen to your tissues and cells with greater efficiency. Regular aerobic exercise will reduce stress and increase your stamina. Common aerobic exercises include running or jogging, freestyle swimming, aerobics classes, vigorous cycling, and brisk walking.

Beyond aerobic fitness, you may have other objectives in taking up exercise. If increased muscle strength is important, you may want to include weight lifting or isometric exercise in your program. (If you have a heart condition or angina, you should probably not engage in weight lifting or bodybuilding.) Exercise that involves stretching, such as dancing or yoga, is ideal for developing muscular flexibility and is a good complement to aerobic exercise. If you want to lose weight, jogging or cycling are probably most effective. If discharging aggression and frustration is important, you might try competitive sports.

Finally, if you just want to get out into nature, then hiking or gardening would be appropriate. Rigorous hiking (as done by the Sierra Club, for example) can increase both strength and endurance.

Many people find it helpful to vary the type of exercise they do. Doing two or more different forms of exercise on alternate days is sometimes referred to as "cross training." This gives you the opportunity to develop a more balanced state of fitness by exercising different muscle groups. Popular combinations involve doing an aerobic type of exercise such as jogging or cycling three to four times a week and a socializing exercise (such as golf), or a bodybuilding exercise, twice a week. Maintaining a program with two distinct types of exercise prevents either from becoming too boring.

What follows are brief descriptions of some of the more common types of aerobic exercise. Each type has its advantages and possible drawbacks.

Running

For many years, jogging or running has been the most popular form of aerobic exercise, perhaps because of its convenience. The only equipment you need is running shoes, and in many cases you need only step out your door to begin. Running is one of the best forms of exercise for losing weight, as it burns calories quickly. Numerous studies have shown its benefits for depression, as it raises both endorphin and serotonin levels in the brain. Running decreases anxiety by metabolizing excess adrenaline and releasing skeletal muscle tension. A three-mile jog (approximately thirty minutes) four or five times per week can go a long way toward diminishing your vulnerability to anxiety. Work up to a pace of one mile every twelve minutes.

The downside to running is that, over a period of time, it can increase your risk of injury. In particular, if you run on hard surfaces, the constant shock to your joints can lead to foot, knee, or back problems. You can minimize your risk of injury by:

- Getting proper shoes—those that minimize shock to your joints.

- Running on soft surfaces—preferably grass, dirt, a track, or a hardened beach. Avoid concrete if possible; asphalt is okay if you have good shoes and don't run every day.

- Warming up before you begin. Try doing a minute or two of very slow jogging.

- Alternating jogging with other forms of exercise. Avoid jogging every day.

If running outdoors is a problem because of weather, lack of a soft surface, smog, or traffic, you may want to invest in an automatic treadmill. To make this less boring, put it in front of your TV or VCR.

Swimming

Swimming is an especially good exercise because it uses so many different muscles throughout the body. Doctors usually recommend swimming to people with musculoskeletal problems, injuries, or arthritis, because it minimizes shock to the joints. It does not promote weight loss to the same degree as running, but it will help firm up your body.

For aerobic-level conditioning, it's best to swim freestyle for twenty to thirty minutes, preferably four or five times per week. For moderate, relaxing exercise, breaststroke is an enjoyable alternative. As a rule, it's best to work out in a heated pool where the water temperature is seventy-five to eighty degrees.

The major downside with swimming is that many pools are heavily chlorinated. This may be quite irritating to your eyes, skin, or hair—as well as the membranes in your upper respiratory passages. You can counter some of this by wearing goggles and a nose plug. If you're fortunate, you may be able to find a pool that uses hydrogen peroxide or bubbled-in ozone as a disinfectant. If the pool you use is chlorinated, it's a good idea to soap off in a shower afterward.

Cycling

Cycling has become a very popular form of aerobic exercise in recent years. While having many of the same benefits as jogging, it's less damaging to your joints. To achieve aerobic conditioning, cycling needs to be done vigorously—approximately fifteen miles per hour or more on a flat surface. When the weather is good, cycling can be quite enjoyable—especially if you have beautiful surroundings with little traffic or a designated bike trail. If weather precludes cycling, you need a stationary bike indoors, possibly in front of your TV or VCR.

If you want to take up outdoor cycling, you'll need to make an initial investment in a good bike. You may want to borrow someone else's bike until you feel ready to spend several hundred dollars. Make sure the bike you purchase is designed and sized correctly for your body, or it may cause you problems. A well-cushioned seat is a good investment.

When you undertake cycling, give yourself a few months to work up to a fifteen-miles-per-hour cruising speed, that is, a mile every four minutes. One hour of cycling three to five times per week is sufficient. Be sure to wear a helmet and try to avoid riding at night.

Aerobics Classes

Most aerobics classes consist of warm-up stretches and aerobic exercises led by an instructor. These are usually done to music. Classes are generally offered by health clubs, with various levels for beginning, intermediate, and advanced participants. Since certain of the exercises can be traumatic to joints, try to find a "low-impact" aerobics class. The structured format of an aerobics class may be an excellent way to motivate you to exercise. If you are self-motivated and prefer to stay at home, there are many good aerobics videos available.

If you decide to do aerobic exercises, be sure to obtain good shoes that stabilize your feet, absorb shock, and minimize twisting. It's best to do these exercises on a wooden surface and to avoid thick carpets, if possible. About forty-five minutes to an hour of exercise (including warm-up) three to five times per week is sufficient.

Walking

Walking has advantages over all other forms of exercise. First, it does not require training—you already know how to do it. Second, it requires no equipment other than a pair of shoes and can be done virtually anywhere—even in a shopping mall if necessary. The chances of injury are less than for any other type of exercise. Finally, it's the most natural form of activity. All of us are naturally inclined to walk. Up until society became sedentary, it was a natural part of life.

Walking for relaxation and distraction is one thing; doing it for aerobic conditioning is another. To make walking aerobic, aim for about one hour at a brisk enough pace to cover three miles. A twenty- or thirty-minute walk is generally not enough to obtain aerobic-level conditioning. If you make walking your regular form of exercise, do it four to five times per week, preferably outdoors. If you feel an hour of brisk walking is not enough of a workout, try adding hand weights or finding an area with hills. Indoor treadmills can be adjusted to make walking aerobic.

To get the most benefit out of walking, good posture is important. If it feels natural to allow your arms to swing opposite to the stride of your legs, you'll be getting "cross-lateral conditioning," which helps to integrate the left and right hemispheres of your brain. Good walking shoes are also important. Look for padded insoles, a good arch, and firm support of the heel.

Once you can comfortably walk three or four miles without stopping, consider taking hiking trips—day or overnight—

in county, state, or national parks. Hiking outdoors can revitalize your soul as much as it does your body.

Exercise Your Right to Have Fun

Exercise should be interesting and fun; it's important that you make it interesting early on so that you keep it up. There are several ways to do this. If you're not limited to being indoors, try to get outside, preferably in an attractive natural setting such as a park or, even better, the countryside. If you're doing a solo-type exercise such as swimming, cycling, or jogging, see if you can find a companion to go with you at least sometimes. If you need to exercise indoors because of personal limitations or climate, play music or watch a video while you're on your stationary bike or treadmill. Some people actually learn foreign languages while exercising!

Don't Be Undermined by Excuses

Do you notice a sudden boost in your creative powers when it comes to making excuses for not exercising? If so, you're not alone, but that doesn't mean you should succumb to these excuses and let them undermine your resolve. Below is a list of common excuses for avoiding exercise and ways to counter them.

"I don't have enough time." What you are really saying is that you're not willing to make time. You aren't assigning enough importance to the increased fitness, well-being, and improved control over anxiety you will surely gain from exercise. The problem is not a matter of time but one of priorities.

"I feel too tired to exercise." One solution is to exercise before going to work—or on your lunch break—rather than at the end of the day. If this is simply impossible, don't give up. What many nonexercisers fail to realize is that moderate exercise can actually *overcome* fatigue. Many people exercise *in spite* of feeling tired and find that they feel rejuvenated and reenergized afterward. Things will grow easier once you get past the initial inertia of starting to exercise.

"Exercise is boring—it's no fun." Is it really true that *all* the activities listed earlier are boring to you? Have you tried out all of them? It may be that you need to find someone to exercise with in order to have more fun. Or perhaps you need to go back and forth between two different types of exercise to stimulate your interest. Exercise can begin to feel wonderful after a few months when it becomes *inherently* rewarding, even if it seemed difficult initially.

"It's too inconvenient to go out somewhere to exercise." This is really no problem, as there are several ways to get vigorous exercise in the comfort of your home. Stationary bicycles and powered treadmills have become very popular, and twenty minutes per day on one will give you a good workout. If this seems boring, try listening to a portable CD or tape player with headphones or place your stationary bike or treadmill in front of the TV. Aerobic exercise at home is convenient and fun if you have a VCR. Jane Fonda's low-impact aerobics video is a good one to start out with. Other indoor activities include jumping on a rebounder, calisthenics, using a rowing machine, or using a universal gym with adjustable weights. There are also early-morning exercise programs on TV. If you can't afford exercise equipment or a VCR, just put on some wild music and dance for twenty minutes. In short, it is quite possible to maintain an adequate exercise program without leaving your home.

"Exercise causes a buildup of lactic acid—doesn't that cause panic attacks?" It is true that exercise increases the production of lactic acid, and that lactic acid can promote panic attacks in some people who are already prone to them. However, regular exercise also increases *oxygen turnover* in your body. Oxygen turnover is the capacity of your body to oxidize substances it doesn't need, including lactic acid. Any increase in lactic acid produced by exercise will be offset by your body's increased capacity to remove it.

The net effect of regular exercise is an overall *reduction* in your body's tendency to accumulate lactic acid.

"I'm over forty—and that's too old to start exercising." Unless your doctor gives you a clear medical reason for not exercising, age is never a valid excuse. With patience and persistence, it is possible to get into excellent physical shape at almost any age.

"I'm too overweight and out of shape," or "I'm afraid I'll have a heart attack if I stress my body by exercising vigorously." *If you have physical reasons to worry about stressing your heart, be sure to design your exercise program with the help of your physician.* Vigorous walking is a safe exercise for virtually everyone, and is considered by some physicians to be the ideal exercise, as it rarely causes muscle or bone injuries. Swimming is also a safe bet if you're out of shape or overweight. Be sensible and realistic in the exercise program you choose. The important thing is to be consistent and committed, whether your program involves walking for one hour every day or training for a marathon.

"I've tried exercise once and it didn't work." The question to ask here is why it didn't work. Did you start off too hard and fast? Did you get bored? Did you balk at the initial aches and pains? Did you feel lonely exercising by yourself? Perhaps it is time for you to give yourself another chance to discover all the physical and psychological benefits of a regular exercise program.

Regular exercise is an essential component of the total program for overcoming anxiety, worry, and phobias presented in this book. If you combine regular, aerobic exercise with a program of regular, deep relaxation, you are undoubtedly going to experience a substantial reduction in generalized anxiety. Exercise and deep relaxation are the two methods *most effective* for altering a hereditary-biochemical predisposition to anxiety—that part of your anxiety that you came equipped with, rather than learned.

Eat Right to
Stay Calm

By the end of this chapter ...
   You will know how to:
   - Taper off of caffeine
   - Minimize your sugar intake and manage hypoglycemia
   - Choose a relaxing herb

Grounds for Anxiety

Caffeine consumption, particularly in the form of coffee drinking, is endemic to our culture and is even something of a rite of passage. For many, a reliance on "that morning cup of coffee" is a milestone on the way to maturity and may coincide with the onset of adult responsibilities. But while it is often viewed as a coping aid, caffeine in all its forms can spur physiological states that precipitate anxiety. Indeed, of all the dietary culprits it is the most notorious. Caffeine increases the level of the neurotransmitter norepinephrine in your brain, which leaves you alert and awake, and it heightens sympathetic nervous system activity and adrenaline output in the same way that stress does. Also, caffeine robs you of vitamin B_1 (thiamine), which is one of the so-called antistress vitamins. In short, too much caffeine can keep you in a chronically tense, aroused condition, leaving you more vulnerable to anxiety.

How Much Is Too Much?

As a general rule, you should reduce your total caffeine consumption to *less than 100 milligrams per day* to minimize its anxiety-stimulating effect. This translates into one cup of percolated coffee or one diet cola beverage, at most, per day.

Keep in mind, though, that there are tremendous individual differences in sensitivity to caffeine. There are those who can down five cups of coffee a day with minimal effects, while at the opposite extreme are people who become jittery after a single cola or cup of tea. As with any addictive drug, chronic caffeine consumption leads to increased tolerance and a potential for withdrawal symptoms. If you have been drinking five cups of coffee a day and abruptly cut down to one a day, you may have withdrawal reactions including fatigue, depression, and headaches. It's better to taper off gradually over a period of several months. For example, from five cups to four cups per day for a month, then two or three cups per day for the next month, and so on. Some people like to substitute decaffeinated coffee, which has about four milligrams of caffeine per cup, while others substitute herbal teas. So you should do a little experimenting to find out what your own optimal daily caffeine intake might be. For most people prone to anxiety, this turns out to be less than 100 milligrams per day. If you have panic attacks you may want to cut out caffeine altogether.

Caffeine Content of Some Commonly Used Products

Hot Beverage	Caffeine per Cup
Coffee, drip	146 mg
Coffee, instant	66 mg
Coffee, percolated	110 mg
Cocoa	13 mg
Decaffeinated coffee	4 mg
Loose tea, five-minute brew	40 mg
Teabag, five-minute brew	46 mg
Teabag, one-minute brew	28 mg

Soft Drink	Caffeine per 12-Ounce Can
Coca-Cola	65 mg
Diet Dr. Pepper	54 mg
Dr. Pepper	61 mg
Mountain Dew	55 mg
Pepsi-Cola	43 mg
Tab	49 mg

Over-the-Counter Drug	Caffeine per Tablet
Anacin	32 mg
Caffedrine	200 mg
Empirin	32 mg
Excedrin	65 mg
Midol	132 mg
No-Doz	100 mg
Vanquish	33 mg
Vivarin	200 mg

Other	
Chocolate	25 mg per candy bar

Sugar Doesn't Sweeten the Deal

Do you believe in reincarnation? If you do, we can tell you one thing for sure about your past lives: unless you were born into vast wealth, you would not have had the opportunity to consume much sugar. Certainly, you wouldn't have devoured the 120 *pounds* of it per year that the average American consumes.

The rising intake of sugar began in the twentieth century and has reached an unprecedented height in present-day America. One or two desserts and sugar-laden snacks have become regular features of our daily diet. In addition, sugar is found in everything from salad dressings to processed meat to cereal and in many beverages.

The Sugar Roller Coaster

Because our bodies are not equipped to rapidly process large doses of sugar, a chronic imbalance in sugar metabolism often results. For some, this means high levels of blood sugar, or diabetes, the prevalence of which has skyrocketed in our time. For many more, though, the problem is the exact opposite: periodic dips in blood sugar that trigger a condition called *hypoglycemia.*

Low Blood Sugar, High Anxiety

The symptoms of hypoglycemia tend to appear when your blood sugar drops below fifty to sixty milligrams per milliliter or when it drops suddenly from a higher to a lower level. Typically this occurs about two to three hours after eating a meal. It can also occur *simply in response to stress,* since your body burns up sugar very rapidly under stress. The most common symptoms of hypoglycemia are:

- light-headedness
- nervousness

- trembling

- feelings of unsteadiness or weakness

- irritability

- palpitations

Do the symptoms sound familiar? All of them are also anxiety symptoms! In fact, for some, anxiety reactions may actually be caused by hypoglycemia. Generally, the anxiety recedes after having something to eat, which causes blood sugar to rise. An informal, nonclinical way to diagnose hypoglycemia is to determine whether you have any of the above symptoms three or four hours after a meal, and whether they then go away as soon as you have something to eat.

Blood sugar plummets when the pancreas releases an excess of insulin. Insulin is a hormone that causes sugar in the bloodstream to be taken up by the cells. (This is why it is used in the treatment of diabetes to lower excessive blood sugar levels.) In hypoglycemia the pancreas tends to overshoot in its production of insulin. If you ingest too much sugar, you may have a temporary sugar high followed half an hour later by a crash when your body produces a lot of insulin.

This can also happen in response to sudden or chronic stress. Stress can cause a rapid depletion of blood sugar. You then experience confusion, anxiety, spaciness, and tremulousness because your brain is not getting enough sugar and a secondary stress response occurs.

When blood sugar falls too low, your adrenal glands kick in and release adrenaline and cortisol, which causes you to feel more anxious and aroused. This has the specific purpose of causing your liver to release stored sugar to bring your blood sugar level back to normal. So the subjective symptoms of hypoglycemia arise from both a deficit of blood sugar and a secondary stress response mediated by the adrenal glands.

Getting the Jump on Hypoglycemia

How do you deal with hypoglycemia? Fortunately, it's quite possible to overcome problems with low blood sugar by making several dietary changes and taking certain supplements.

If you suspect that you have hypoglycemia or have had it formally diagnosed, you may want to implement the following guidelines. Doing so may result in less generalized anxiety and increased feelings of serenity. You may also notice that you are less prone to depression and mood swings.

Dietary Modifications for Hypoglycemia

- Eliminate, as much as possible, all types of simple sugar from your diet. This includes foods that obviously contain white sugar, such as candy, ice cream, desserts, and soda. It also includes subtler forms of sugar, such as dextrose, maltose, honey, high fructose corn syrup, corn sweeteners, molasses, and high fructose. Be sure to read labels on all processed foods to detect these various forms of sugar.

- Substitute fruits (other than dried fruits, which are too concentrated in sugar) for sweets. Avoid fruit juices or dilute them with an equal amount of water.

- Reduce or eliminate simple starches such as pasta, refined cereals, potato chips, white rice, and white bread. Substitute instead complex carbohydrates such as whole-grain breads and cereals, vegetables, and brown rice or other whole grains.

- Have a complex carbohydrate and protein snack (tuna and crakers or whole-grain toast and cheese, for example) halfway between meals around 10:30 to 11:00 A.M. and especially around 4:00 to 5:00 P.M. If you awaken at 4:00 or 5:00 A.M., you may also find that a small snack will help you to get back to sleep for a couple of hours. As an alternative to snacks between meals, you can try having four or five small meals per day no more than two to three hours apart. The point of either of these alternatives is to maintain a steadier blood sugar level.

Supplements

Vitamin B-complex, vitamin C, and chelated chromium (such as chromium picolinate, often called glucose tolerance factor) can also help stabilize blood sugar. Vitamin B-complex and vitamin C are useful in increasing your resilience to stress. The B vitamins also help regulate the metabolic processes which convert carbohydrates to sugar in your body. Chromium has a direct, stabilizing effect on your blood sugar level. Below are guidelines for taking these supplements.

Vitamin B-complex. 25–100 milligrams of all eleven B vitamins once per day with a meal.

Vitamin C. 1,000 milligrams once or twice per day with meals.

Organic trivalent chromium (chromium picolinate). 200 micrograms per day. This is available at your local health food store.

Refer to the Resources section for suggested reading on hypoglycemia.

Move Your Diet toward Vegetarianism

A dietary change toward vegetarianism can promote a calmer, less anxiety-prone disposition. If you're used to eating meat, dairy, cheese, and egg products, it is not necessary, or even advisable, to give up all sources of animal protein from your diet. Giving up red meat alone, for example, or restricting your consumption of cow's milk (and using soy or rice milk instead) can have a noticeable and beneficial effect.

How can vegetarianism lead to a calmer disposition? Meat, poultry, dairy, cheese, and egg products, along with sugar and refined flour products, are all *acid-forming foods*. These foods are not necessarily acid in composition, but they leave an acid residue in the body after they are metabolized, making the body itself more acid. This can create two kinds of problems:

1. When the body is more acid, the transit time of food through the digestive tract can increase to the point where vitamins and minerals are not adequately assimilated. This selective underabsorption of vitamins, especially B vitamins, vitamin C, and minerals, can subtly add to the body's stress load and eventually lead to low-grade malnutrition. Taking supplements will not necessarily correct this condition unless you are able to adequately digest and absorb them.

2. Acid-forming foods, especially meats, can create metabolic breakdown products which are congestive to the body. This is especially true if you are already under stress and unable to properly digest protein foods. The result is that you tend to end up feeling more sluggish, tired, and may have excess mucus or sinus problems. Although it's true that this congestion is not exactly the same thing as anxiety, it can certainly add stress to the body, which in turn aggravates tension and anxiety. The more free your body is from congestion due to acid-forming foods, the lighter and more clearerheaded you are likely to feel. Be aware, also, that many medications have an acid reaction in the body and may lead to the same types of problems as acid-forming foods.

To maintain a proper acid-alkaline balance in the body, it helps to decrease consumption of acid-forming foods. Most animal-based foods, sugar, and refined flour products are acid-forming and increase the acidity in your body. Prominent among alkaline foods are all vegetables, most fruits (except plums, raisins, and prunes), whole grains such as brown rice, millet, and buckwheat, and bean sprouts. Ideally, about 50–60 percent of the calories you consume should come from these foods, although in the winter it is okay to eat a slightly higher percentage of animal proteins. Try including more of the alkaline foods in your diet and see if it makes a difference in the way you feel. Increasing the number of alkaline-forming foods in your diet should not lead you to reduce your protein intake.

Increase the Amount of Protein Relative to Carbohydrate You Eat

Until recently most nutritionists advocated eating a high amount of complex carbohydrates (for example, whole grains, pastas, and bread)—as much as 70 percent of total calories. The prevailing idea was that too much fat promoted cardiovascular disease and too much protein led to excessive acidity and toxicity in the body. The ideal diet was thought to consist of 15–20 percent fat, 15–20 percent protein, and the rest carbohydrates.

In the past few years, however, evidence has mounted against the idea of eating high quantities of carbohydrates. Carbohydrates are used by the body to produce sugar or glucose, the form of sugar the body and brain use for fuel. In order to transport glucose to the cells, your pancreas secretes insulin. Eating high levels of carbohydrates means your body produces higher levels of insulin, and too much insulin has an adverse effect on some of the body's most basic hormonal and neuroendocrine systems, especially those that produce prostaglandins and serotonin.

In short, eating high amounts of sweets, cereals, breads, pastas, or even grains (such as rice) or starchy vegetables (such as carrots, corn, and potatoes) can raise your insulin levels to the point that other basic systems are thrown out of balance. The answer is not to eliminate complex carbohydrates but to reduce them *proportionately* to the amounts of protein and fat you consume, *without increasing the total number of calories in your diet.* By doing this, you will not end up eating a diet that is too high in fat or protein. Instead, you will continue to eat fats and protein in moderation *while decreasing the amount of carbohydrate you have each meal relative to fat and protein.* The optimal ratio may be 30 percent protein, 30 percent fat, and 40 percent carbohydrate, with *vegetable* sources of protein and fat preferable to animal sources.

Considerable research supporting the value of reducing the proportion of carbohydrate relative to protein and fat is presented by Dr. Barry Sears in *The Zone* (1995). Anxiety and mood disorders often involve deficiencies in neurotransmitters, especially serotonin. The body has no way to make neurotransmitters (and serotonin in particular) without a steady supply of amino acids, which are derived from protein. Whether or not you agree with Dr. Sears's approach or choose to adopt a 40:30:30 diet, I highly recommend you have some protein (preferably in the form of fish, organic poultry, tofu, tempeh, protein powder, or beans and grains) at every meal. On the other hand, aim not to exceed 30 percent protein—especially in the form of meat, chicken, or fish—as this may tend to make your body overly acidic.

Try a Relaxing Herb

Herbs are plant-based medicines that have been an integral part of health care for thousands of years. In fact, about 25 percent of present-day prescription medications are still based on herbs.

Herbal treatments have been very popular in Europe and recently have gained increasing public interest in the United States. Most drugstores now offer an assortment of herbs that can treat conditions ranging from colds to poor memory.

Herbs tend to work more slowly and gently then prescription drugs. If you're used to the rapid and intense effects of a drug like Xanax, you need to be patient with the milder effect of a relaxing herb such as valerian. The principal advantage of herbs is that they work naturally, in harmony with your body, rather than imposing a specific biochemical change, as in the case of drugs.

Several natural herbs can be used to help reduce anxiety. Though not as potent as prescription tranquilizers, they do have a relaxing effect. Kava and valerian are probably the best known and most widely used at present. Other herbs known for their relaxing effects include passionflower, skullcap, hops, gotu kola, and chamomile. Each of these relaxing herbs can be taken individually or in combination with others. Most health food stores and many drugstores offer these herbs in three forms:

- the bulk herb, which can be boiled to make a tea

- capsules or tablets

- liquid extracts, in which the herb is distilled and preserved in alcohol or glycerin, usually in a small bottle with a medicine dropper

You might want to experiment with all three forms to see which you prefer.

While herbal treatments have advantages, it is important to remember that just because they are natural does not mean that they're risk-free. Before trying any of the herbs mentioned below or any other herbal treatments, be sure to consult your physician.

Kava

Kava (or kava kava) is a natural tranquilizer that has become quite popular in the United States in recent years. Many people feel that it is near as potent a relaxer as prescription tranquilizers such as Xanax. Polynesians have used kava for centuries both in ceremonial rituals and as a social relaxer. Small doses produce a sense of well-being, while large doses can produce lethargy, drowsiness, and reduce muscle tension.

It appears from limited research that kava may tone down the activity of the limbic system, particularly the amygdala, which is a brain center associated with anxiety. Detailed neurophysiological effects of kava are not known at this time. Kava's principal advantage over tranquilizers such as Xanax or Klonopin is that it's not addictive. It's also less likely to impair memory or aggravate depression in the way tranquilizers sometimes can.

In buying kava, it is preferable to obtain a standardized extract with a specified percentage of *kavalactones*, the active ingredient. The percentage of kavalactones can vary from 30–70 percent. If you multiply the total number of milligrams of kava in each capsule or tablet by the percentage of kavalactones, you get the actual strength of the dose. For example, a 200-milligram capsule with 70 percent kavalactones would actually be a 140-milligram dose.

Most kava supplements at your health food store contain on the order of 50–70 milligrams kavalactones per capsule. Research has found that taking three or four doses of this strength daily may be as effective as a tranquilizer.

Kava: A Crucial Precaution

Please note: Recently, the herb kava was linked to severe liver damage in a small number of people who took it, mostly in Europe. It is important that you get your doctor's approval before trying kava. Be sure to tell him or her about any medications you are currently taking and any preexisting conditions you may have. Do not take Kava if you have liver problems or are taking medications with known adverse effects on the liver. Avoid combining kava with tranquilizers such as Xanax or Klonopin, as well as with alcohol. Also note that kava is sold under a variety of names, so be sure to find out for certain what is in any herbal supplement before taking it.

Valerian

Valerian is a herbal tranquilizer and sedative that is very widely used in Europe. In recent years it has gained popularity in the United States. Clinical studies, mostly in Europe, have found it to be as effective as tranquilizers in alleviating mild to moderate anxiety and insomnia. Yet it has fewer side effects and is nonaddictive. Valerian is also not as likely as prescription tranquilizers to impair memory and concentration or cause lethargy and drowsiness.

Valerian can be obtained at any health food store in three forms: capsules, liquid extract, or tea. In treating anxiety or insomnia, try each of these forms to see which you like best, following the instructions given on the bottle or package. Frequently you'll find valerian combined with other relaxing herbs such as passionflower, skullcap, hops, or chamomile. You may find these combinations to be more palatable or effective, so try them as well.

Valerian may take a week or so to reach its full effectiveness in treating anxiety or insomnia, so stay with it even if you don't get immediate results. As a general rule, I would not recommend using valerian on a *daily* basis for more than six months. You can use it two to three times per week, however, indefinitely.

Long experience in Europe indicates valerian is an especially safe herb. Still, there are occasional reports of paradoxical reactions of *increased* anxiety, restlessness, or heart palpitations, possibly due to allergy. Stop using valerian or any other herb if it causes such reactions.

Passionflower

Passionflower is a good natural tranquilizer considered by many to be as effective as valerian. In higher doses it is often used to treat insomnia, as it relieves both nervous tension and relaxes muscles. It's available in either capsules or liquid extract at your health food store. Sometimes you'll find products that combine it with valerian or other relaxing herbs. Use it as directed on the bottle or package.

Gotu Kola

Gotu kola has been popular for thousands of years in India. It has a mildly relaxing effect and helps revitalize a weakened nervous system. It has also been found to help improve circulation, memory function, and promote healing following childbirth. You can find it in most health food stores in capsules or extracts.

Nourish Yourself

By the end of this chapter ...
You will know how to:

- Include more downtime in your schedule
- Develop a healthy sleep cycle
- Pace yourself for a more harmonious life

Self-Nourishment Is a Necessity, Not a Luxury

Self-nourishment means maintaining a daily routine of sufficient sleep, recreation, and downtime. It also means pacing yourself through your day to allow time for such things. Taking time for self-nourishment provides you with the energy, presence of mind, and stamina that you need to pursue the activities and goals that make up your life. It also contributes to a calmer, more serene outlook, which is fundamental to reducing anxiety. Because the pace of modern life is frenetic, and often unremitting, this prerequisite to emotional and physical vitality is often overlooked. Some people see self-nourishment as a luxury that they can't readily afford. It is important to remember, though, that self-nourishment is not an optional adjunct to your daily schedule; it is essential to maintaining that schedule.

Take Downtime

Downtime is exactly what it sounds like—time out from work or other responsibilities to give yourself an opportunity to rest and replenish your energy. Without periods of downtime, any stress you experience while dealing with work or other responsibilities tends to become cumulative. It keeps building without any respite. You may tend to keep pushing yourself until finally you drop from exhaustion or experience an aggravation of your anxiety or phobias. Sleep at night doesn't count as downtime. If you go to bed feeling stressed, you may sleep for eight hours and still wake up feeling tense, tired, and stressed. Downtime needs to be scheduled during the day, apart from sleep at night. Its primary purpose is simply to allow a break in the stress cycle to prevent your stress from building. Optimally, you should have the following amounts of downtime:

- one hour per day
- one day per week
- one week out of every twelve to sixteen weeks

If you don't have four weeks of paid vacation per year, try to rearrange your finances so you can take time off without pay. During periods of downtime, disengage from any task you consider work, put aside all responsibilities, and don't answer the phone unless you know it's someone you enjoy hearing from on the other end of the line.

Three Kinds of Downtime

There are three kinds of downtime, each of which is an important factor in developing a more anxiety-free lifestyle: *rest time, recreation time,* and *relationship time.*

Rest Time

Rest time is time when you set aside all activities and just allow yourself to be. You stop action and let yourself fully rest. Rest time might involve lying on the couch and doing nothing, quietly meditating, sitting in your recliner and listening to peaceful music, soaking in your bathtub, or taking a catnap in the middle of the workday. Light reading or TV can pass for rest time, but they are not as helpful as just stopping everything to rest. The key to rest time is that it is fundamentally passive; you allow yourself to stop doing and accomplishing and just be. Contemporary society encourages us to be productive and always accomplish more and more every moment of the waking day. Rest time is a needed counterweight.

Recreation Time

Recreation time involves engaging in activities that help to re-create you, that is, serve to replenish your energy. Recreation time brightens and uplifts your spirit. In essence, it is doing anything that you experience as fun or play. Examples of such activities might include puttering in the garden, reading a novel, seeing a special movie, going on a hike, playing volleyball, taking a short trip, baking a loaf of bread, or fishing. You can take time for recreation during the week, but it is most important to have on your days off from work. Such time can be spent either alone or with someone else, in which case it overlaps with the third type of downtime, relationship time.

Relationship Time

Relationship time is time when you put aside your private goals and responsibilities in order to enjoy being with another person, or, in some cases, with several people. The focus of relationship time is to honor your relationship with your partner, children, extended family members, friends, or pets, and forget about your individual pursuits for a while. If you have a family, relationship time needs to be allocated equitably between time alone with your spouse or partner, time alone with your children, and time when the entire family gets together.

Get Past Workaholism

Workaholism is an addictive disorder characterized by an unhealthy preoccupation with work. Those who suffer from it find that work is the only thing that gives them a sense of inner fulfillment and self-worth. You devote all your time and energy to work, neglecting both your physical and emotional needs. Workaholism produces an unbalanced way of life which often leads first to chronic stress, then to burnout, and potentially to illness.

If you're a workaholic, it's possible to *learn* to enjoy nonwork aspects of your life and achieve a more balanced approach in general. Deliberately making time for rest, recreation, and relationships may be difficult at first, but tends to get easier, and to become self-rewarding, as time goes on.

Be Willing to Do Less

Another important step is simply to be willing to do less. That is, you literally reduce the number of tasks and responsibilities you handle in any given day. In some cases this may involve changing jobs; in others, merely restructuring how you allocate time for work versus rest and relaxation. For some this translates into a fundamental shift in priorities so that maintaining a simple, more balanced lifestyle takes precedence over earning money or gathering accolades. Consider how you can shift your values in the direction of placing more emphasis on the *process* of life (how you live) as opposed to accomplishments and productivity (what you actually do) within your current life situation.

Exercise: How Can You Allow for More Downtime in Your Schedule?

Take some time to reflect on how you might allocate more time for each of the three types of downtime: rest time, recreation time, and relationship time. Write your answers on a piece of paper.

Get a Good Night's Sleep (Regularly)

Healthy sleep patterns are a common casualty of the 24/7 pace of the modern world. To some, a good night's sleep is seen almost as a treat, but sufficient sleep is essential to your overall well-being. Lack of sleep can be both a cause and an effect of anxiety.

Do's and Don'ts of Developing a Healthy Sleep Pattern

It's important to remember that sleep is as integral to physical and mental well-being as proper nutrition and regular exercise. The guidelines below are designed to help you maintain a healthy sleep routine.

Do:

- Exercise during the day. Twenty minutes or more of aerobic exercise midday or in the late afternoon before dinner is optimal. At minimum, forty-five minutes to an hour of brisk walking daily will suffice. Many people find a short walk (twenty to thirty minutes) before bedtime to be helpful.

- Go to bed and get up at regular times. Even if you're tired in the morning, make an effort to stick to your scheduled wake-up time, and don't vary your nightly bedtime. You can resume whatever you're working on or doing the next day. Your body prefers a regular cycle of sleep and wakefulness.

- Develop a sleep ritual before bedtime. This is some activity you do nightly before turning in.

- Reduce noise. Use earplugs or a noise-masking machine, like a fan, if necessary.

- Block out excess light.

- Keep your room temperature between sixty-five and seventy degrees. Too warm or cold a room tends to interfere with sleep. Use fans for a hot room if air conditioning is unavailable. Your room should be ventilated, not stuffy.

- Purchase a quality mattress. Pillows should not be too high or too puffy. Feather pillows, which compress, are best.

- Have separate beds if your partner snores, kicks, or tosses and turns. Discuss this with him or her and decide on a mutually acceptable distance.

- Have physically and emotionally satisfying sex. This often aids sleep.

- See a psychotherapist if necessary. Anxiety and depressive disorders commonly produce insomnia. Talking to a competent psychotherapist can help.

- Turn yourself down during the last hour or two of the day. Avoid vigorous physical or mental activity, emotional upsets, and so on.

- Try a hot shower or bath before bedtime.

Don't:

- Try to force yourself to sleep. If you're unable to fall asleep after twenty to thirty minutes in bed, leave your bed, engage in some relaxing activity (such as watching TV, sitting in a chair and listening to a relaxation tape, meditating, or having a cup of herb tea), and return to bed only when you're sleepy. The same applies for waking up in the middle of the night and having difficulty going back to sleep.

- Have a heavy meal before bedtime or go to bed hungry. A small, healthy snack just before bedtime can be helpful.

- Indulge in heavy alcohol consumption before bedtime. For some people, a small glass of wine before bed may help, but your alcohol consumption should not exceed this.

- Have too much caffeine. Try to limit caffeine intake to the mornings. If you're sensitive to caffeine, avoid it altogether and try decaf coffee or herb teas.

- Smoke cigarettes. Nicotine is a mild stimulant, and apart from its more publicized health risks, it can interfere with sleep. If you are a smoker, talk to your doctor about the best ways to curtail this habit.

- Engage in nonsleep activities in bed. Unless they are part of your sleep ritual, avoid activities such as working or reading in bed. This tends to strengthen the association between bed and sleep.

- Nap during the day. Short catnaps (fifteen to twenty minutes) are okay, but long naps of an hour or more may interfere with sleep the following night.

- Let yourself be afraid of insomnia. Work on *accepting* those nights when you don't sleep so well. You can still function the next day, even if you had only a couple of hours of sleep. The less you fight, resist, or fear sleeplessness, the more it will tend to go away.

A Few Tips for Getting a Good Night's Sleep

- With your doctor's or health practitioner's approval, try natural supplements that foster sleep. Herbs such as kava and valerian, in higher doses, can induce sleep. Do not exceed recommended doses and be sure to discuss all herbs with your doctor before taking them. Some people find 0.5–2 milligrams of the hormone melatonin to be helpful. L-tryptophan, an amino acid that was taken off the market during the 1990s, is currently available. Combined with a carbohydrate snack before bedtime, it is a potent sedative in doses of 1000 milligrams or more. Finally, the amino acid GABA, 500–1000 milligrams before bedtime, may induce sleep. As far as possible, try to avoid using prescription drugs for sleep. They interfere with your sleep cycle and ultimately aggravate insomnia.

- For relaxing tense muscles or a racing mind, use deep relaxation techniques. Specifically, progressive muscle relaxation or taped guided visualization exercises can be helpful (see chapters 1 and 2). Get an autoreverse recorder that can play a tape in a continuous loop.

- Try varying the firmness of your mattress. Invest in a new one or insert a board underneath one that sags or is too soft. For a mattress that is too hard, place an egg-crate foam pad between the mattress surface and the mattress cover.

- If pain is causing sleeplessness, try an analgesic. In the case of pain, this is more appropriate than a sleeping pill.

Pace Yourself and Take Minibreaks

Self-image and personal ideals frequently do not harmonize with the needs of the body. Self-imposed standards regarding work, success, achievement, or how well you take care of others can lead you to betray the natural rhythms of your body. The degree of stress you experience today is a direct measure of how far you've gotten ahead of your body's needs in the past. Pacing yourself and giving yourself small breaks throughout the day are two ways to begin reversing unhealthy trends and living more in harmony with yourself.

Set the Pace That's Right for You

Pacing means living your life at an optimal rate. Too much activity packed into each day, without breaks, leads to exhaustion, stress, anxiety, and perhaps even illness. Not enough activity leads to boredom and self-absorption. Many people with anxiety problems tend to pace themselves too fast, following the lead of a society that tells us to do more, achieve more, and excel no matter what the cost. By looking to external standards, you can impose a pace on yourself that, although others may maintain it, is simply not right for you. Just as you wouldn't buy clothes to fit your neighbor, cousin, or spouse, you shouldn't design a schedule that might work for someone else, but not for you.

Minibreaks

A higher level of relaxation and inner peace requires a schedule that allows for time between activities to rest, reflect, and simply be. If you tend to rush through the activities of your day, experiment with slowing down and giving yourself a five- to ten-minute minibreak every hour or at least every two hours. *Minibreaks can be especially helpful at times when you transition from one activity to another.* For example, after commuting in the morning, take a short break before going into work.

Or after cooking a meal, take a short break before sitting down to eat. During your break, you might practice abdominal breathing, meditate, get up and take a short walk, do a few yoga stretches, or do anything else that helps you to reenergize, relax, and clear your mind. By pacing yourself to allow for short breaks throughout the day, you'll notice a significant difference in the way you feel. You may also be surprised to find that you get just as much or even more done, because you bring more energy and clarity to your activities. Giving yourself short breaks to regroup through the day is simple in principle, though it will require a commitment on your part to practice. You are likely to find it well worth the effort.

Nurture Yourself on a Daily Basis

Although life brings ups and downs—even sudden, unexpected challenges—you can find reprieve from worry and build a sense of inner security through small acts of kindness toward yourself on a daily basis. Doing so requires first that you make time to nurture yourself apart from the responsibilities of work and household. Building a loving relationship with yourself is really not much different from developing a close relationship with someone else: both require some time, energy, and commitment. Giving yourself regular downtime is one way to do this. The following list offers a number of other simple, self-nurturing activities. When outer life circumstances seem harsh, it's particularly important to make time for yourself without feeling guilty or self-indulgent.

Read an Uplifting Book

One way you can unwind and restore your spirit is to read an uplifting book. This can be an inspiring novel, a forward-looking self-help book, or perhaps a book focusing on spiritual themes. As you enter the author's world through the book, you can move into a different mental space with relatively little effort. Sometimes it takes reading only a few pages to raise your consciousness to a higher track. See the Resources section for a list of recommended books.

Take Time for Sensual Pleasures

Take a warm bath.

Take a sauna.

Get a massage.

Take a bubble bath.

Have a manicure or pedicure.

Sit in a hot tub.

If it's cold outdoors, sit by an indoor fire.

Cuddle with a special person.

Revel in the World around You

Go for a scenic walk.

Take time to watch the sunrise or sunset.

Sleep outside under the stars.

Go to a park (or lake, beach, or the mountains).

Have Fun

Rent a funny video.

Eat at a good restaurant.

Play your favorite music and dance to it.

Call a good friend or several good friends.

Buy some new clothes.

Buy yourself something special that you can afford.

See a good film or show.

Browse in a book or music store for as long as you want.

Visit a museum or other interesting place.

Work on your favorite puzzle or puzzle book.

Buy yourself flowers.

Write a letter to an old friend.

Bake or cook something special.

Go window-shopping.

Play with your pet.

Do Something Just for You

Relax with a good book, magazine, or soothing music.

Go to bed early.

Take a mental health day off from work.

Fix a special dinner just for yourself and eat it by candlelight.

Have a cup of your favorite herb tea.

Meditate.

Write yourself an upbeat letter and mail it.

Give yourself more time than you need to accomplish whatever you're doing. Let yourself dawdle.

Read an inspirational book.

Listen to a positive, motivational tape.

Write in a special diary about your reflections, insights, and accomplishments.

Have breakfast in bed.

Simplify Your Life

By the end of this chapter ...
    You will know how to:

- Simplify your life by making short- and long-term changes

Keep It Simple

Having a life that is freighted with onerous financial and time commitments, as well as excessive material items, is a modern source of anxiety. Although this kind of excess is characteristic of our time, it remains true that the simpler our lives, the richer our experience and the deeper our sense of well-being.

Simplicity is not to be mistaken for austerity. An austere life is mired in deprivation and want, while a simple life is rewarding, creative, and nourishing to the spirit. The simple life is free of those demands on your time and finances that deplete your resources without enriching your life in some way. It can be thought of as a lifestyle that yields a better return on your investment of time and money. A common misconception about simplicity is that it means doing away with modern comforts and conveniences to prove your ability to live apart from twentieth-century technology. Gandhi made a telling statement about denying the material side of life: "As long as you derive inner help and comfort from anything, you should keep it. If you were to give it up in a mood of self-sacrifice or out of a stern sense of duty, you would continue to want it back, and that unsatisfied want would make trouble for you."

One View of the Simple Life

There is no precise formula defining what constitutes living simply. Each individual is likely to discover his or her own ways to reduce complexity and unnecessary encumbrances. In his 1993 book *Voluntary Simplicity*, Duane Elgin suggests that people who choose to simplify their lives:

- invest the time and energy freed up by simpler living in activities with their partners, children, and friends (for example, walking, making music together, sharing a meal, or camping)

- work on developing the full spectrum of their potentials: physical (running, biking, hiking, and so on), emotional (learning the skills of intimacy and sharing feelings in important relationships), mental (engaging in lifelong learning by reading and taking classes), and spiritual (learning to move through life with a quiet mind and compassionate heart)

- tend to feel an intimate connection with the earth and a reverential concern for nature

- feel a compassionate concern for the world's poor

- lower their overall level of personal consumption— buying less clothing, for example, with more attention to what is functional, durable, and aesthetic, and less concern with passing fads, fashions, and seasonal styles

- alter their patterns of consumption in favor of products that are durable, easy to repair, nonpolluting in their manufacture and use, energy-efficient, functional, and aesthetic

- shift their diet away from highly processed foods, meat, and sugar, toward foods that are more natural, healthy, and simple

- reduce undue clutter and complexity by giving away or selling those possessions that are seldom used and could be used productively by others (clothing, books, furniture, appliances, tools, and so on)

- recycle metal, glass, and paper and cut back on consumption of items that are wasteful of nonrenewable resources

- develop skills that contribute to greater self-reliance and reduce dependence upon experts to handle life's ordinary demands (basic carpentry, plumbing, and appliance repair)

- prefer smaller-scale, more human-sized living and working environments that foster a sense of community, face-to-face contact, and mutual caring

- participate in holistic health-care practices that emphasize preventative medicine and the healing powers of the body when assisted by the mind

- change transportation modes in favor of public transit, carpooling, smaller and more fuel-efficient autos, living closer to work, riding a bike, and walking

If anything, a simpler life gives you more *time* to foster connections with your family, community, nature, and Higher Power, as well as with yourself. Nothing in nature is isolated—it's only the abstract, conceptual mind that creates distinctions and separations. When you allow yourself to experience the various levels of relatedness that are natural or "indigenous" to life, you begin to overcome separation in all of its manifestations and heal the problem of anxiety at its roots.

There have been indications in recent years that an increasing number of people have favored simplifying their lives. After thirty years of economic expansion and material growth, the decade of the nineties was, for many, a time of downsizing. According to a survey conducted in 1991 and quoted by Elgin in *Voluntary Simplicity* (1995):

- 69 percent of the people surveyed said they would like to "slow down and live a more relaxed life," in contrast to only 19 percent who said they would like to "live a more exciting, faster-paced life"

- 61 percent agreed that "earning a living today requires so much effort that it's difficult to find time to enjoy life"

- when asked about their priorities, 89 percent said it was more important these days to spend time with their families

- only 13 percent saw importance in keeping up with fashion trends and just 7 percent thought it was worth bothering to shop for status-symbol products

A poll published in June 1997 in *USA Today* reported that in 1995, 28 percent of Americans said they had deliberately made life changes during the preceding five years that resulted in less income, with 87 percent of them reporting satisfaction with the change.

Some Ways to Simplify Your Life

Below are a few suggestions for simplifying your life. Some are changes you can make immediately, while others require more time and effort on your part. Remember that the goal of the simple life is to free yourself from those commitments that deplete your time, energy, and money without meeting your essential needs or sustaining your spirit.

Downsize Your Living Situation

There are several benefits of smaller living quarters. First, it is just not possible to accumulate a large number of possessions without sufficient room for them. Also, a smaller space takes less time to clean and maintain and is typically less expensive.

Let Go of Things You Don't Need

We live in a time of unprecedented abundance. It's easy to accumulate stuff that has no real value or use to us and only creates clutter. Take a look at your stuff and decide what is useful and worth keeping and what is simply taking up space. As a general rule, to reduce clutter, get rid of everything you haven't used in more than a year, except, of course, items that have sentimental value.

Do What You Want for a Living

Doing what you truly want may require time, risk, and effort. It may take one to two years to gain the retraining or retooling you need to begin a new career. Then you may have to endure some time at an entry-level position before your new line of work meets your financial needs. In our estimation—and that of others who have done it—the time, effort, and disruption are well worth it.

Reduce Your Commute

Reducing or eliminating your commute is one of the most significant changes you can make in simplifying your life. It doesn't take much reflection to see the extent to which negotiating rush hour traffic on a daily basis can add to stress. Moving closer to where you work or choosing to live in a smaller town can help reduce your commute. At the very least, if you have to commute over a long distance, you can try to arrange for flexible hours (to avoid rush hour) or have a comfortable car with a stereo. At this time, nearly 15 percent of Americans work out of their homes, and the number is rising. If you can figure out a consulting service or computer-based job you can do out of your home, you can join them.

Reduce Exposure to TV

How much time during the day do you spend in front of a screen? In the nineties, the average household had two to three TVs, each with an average of forty to sixty channels. As if this were not enough, fifty million American households have computers offering an endless array of child and adult games as well as Internet access to thousands of topics and millions of Web sites. Granted, there are many good programs on TV, and the Internet is a wonderful tool for communicating information. The concern is with the sheer complexity of having so many options, all of which involve a passive stance of either witnessing entertainment or absorbing information. While life in front of the screen can be a distraction from anxiety, it can also be a hindrance to rebuilding a deeper connection with nature, others, or yourself. If anxiety is aggravated by too much stimulation and an experience of disconnection on multiple levels, then it seems that spending time in front of the screen might be done in moderation.

Live Close to Nature

Anxiety states are often associated with feelings of disembodiment. Being ungrounded and out of touch with your feelings and physical body is especially evident in the sensations of depersonalization or derealization that can accompany acute anxiety or panic. This disconnection can be aggravated in situations that involve being literally disconnected from the earth, such as riding in a car, being high up in a tall building, or flying. It may also be aggravated in situations where you are bombarded with so many stimuli that your awareness is scattered, such as a grocery store, shopping mall, or social gathering.

Taking a walk in the woods or a park is a simple act that can help reverse the tendency to feel disembodied. Being in close proximity to the earth—its sights, sounds, smells, and energies—can help you to remain more easily connected with yourself. Choosing to live in such a setting, if possible, allows you to reestablish an ongoing connection with the earth that much of modern civilization seems to have lost.

Tame the Telephone

There are people who feel they should answer the phone virtually every time it rings, regardless of the time of day or the mood they're in at the time. Whether the caller is a creditor, a sales solicitation, or a cantankerous relative, some people feel it is an almost sacred obligation to answer every call. Remember that answering the telephone is optional. You can let your voice mail or answering machine pick up, and return the call when you are ready to give the caller your full attention. If you're engaged in a project or activity that you find rewarding, there's no need to drop it to take a call that does not require your immediate attention.

Delegate Menial Chores

How many menial chores would you delegate to someone else if money were not an issue? Even delegating one activity you don't like to do, such as housecleaning or yard work, can make a difference in the sense of ease you bring to your day-to-day life. If money is an issue, is there something your children could learn to do just about as well as you? Perhaps you can allow other family members to help with the cooking, yard upkeep, or housecleaning.

Learn to Say No

"No" is not a dirty word. Many people pride themselves on always being able to accommodate the needs and wants of their friends, family, and coworkers. The problem is that the end result of this consistent "helpfulness" is exhaustion. You can become so busy taking care of others' wants and needs that you have no time or energy to take care of your own. When someone asks you for your time, effort, or anything else, think about whether it serves both your highest interest and the other person's highest interest to respond with a "yes."

Other Ways to Simplify

There are many other ways you might choose to simplify your life. For example, you can reduce the amount of junk mail you receive by writing to an organization called Stop The Mail at P.O. Box 9008, Farmingdale, NY 11735. Request that your name not be sold to mailing list companies, and you will likely reduce your junk mail by up to 75 percent. Or you can eliminate all of your credit cards except for one. Having one card comes in handy for making purchases over the telephone or Internet or renting a car. Apart from that, you will save yourself a lot of monthly bills as well as annual fees by reducing your number of credit cards.

See the Resources section for suggested books on simplifying your life.

Exercise: Simplify–Your–Life Questionnaire

Now it's your turn. Take some time to think about ways in which you might simplify your life. To help you do this, ask yourself the following questions.

1. On a 1-to-10 scale, with 1 representing a high degree of simplicity and 10 representing a high degree of complexity, where would you rate your own lifestyle at present?

2. Have you made any changes in your living arrangements in the past year toward simplicity? If so, what changes?

3. What changes toward simplifying your life would you like to make in general?

4. What changes toward simplifying your life are you *willing* to make in the next year?

Exercise: Checklist for Living Simply

Review the following simplification strategies and check off or underline the ones you would be willing to try or initiate in the next two months.

o Reduce the clutter in your home

o Move to a smaller house

o Move to a smaller town

o Move close to shopping resources so you can do all of your errands quickly

o Buy less clothing, with attention to what is functional, durable, and aesthetic—rather than trendy

o Drive a simple, fuel-efficient car

o Reduce dependence on your TV

o Reduce dependence on outside entertainment (movies, plays, theater, concerts, nightclubs)

o Reduce (or eliminate) magazine subscriptions

o Stop newspaper delivery

o Stop junk mail

o Stop answering the phone whenever it rings

o Reduce your commute (if possible, walk or ride your bike to work)

o Work where you live

o Tell everyone but your immediate family you no longer do Christmas gifts (or cards, for that matter)

o Take one suitcase if you vacation and pack only essential clothes

o Take your vacation near or at home

o Reduce your consumption to avoid luxury or designer items; favor products that are durable, easy to repair, and nonpolluting

o Take steps to get out of debt

o Keep only one credit card

o Consolidate your bank accounts

o Delegate busywork like yard work, housecleaning, and tax preparation

o Simplify your eating habits to include whole, unprocessed foods

o Buy groceries less often, in bulk

o Make water your drink of choice

o Pack your own lunch

o Learn to say no

o Stop trying to change people

o Stop trying to please people—be yourself

o Dispose of all personal possessions you don't really need

o Do what you truly want for a living

o Work less and spend more time with your loved ones

Some of these changes can be done quickly; others involve a process. It may take a year or two, for example, to arrange your life so that you're doing something you truly enjoy for a living. To dispose of unnecessary possessions, put aside things you think you won't need for a year in a locked closet or storage compartment. At the end of the year, if you've not given them any thought throughout the entire time, let them go. Learning to say no or to stop always trying to please other people requires that you develop assertiveness skills, which you can acquire through classes, workshops, counseling, and books.

We hope this chapter has given you some ideas about how to reduce the complexity in your life. Simplifying your life will give you more time and ability to find peace of mind and appreciate the beauty of life.

Turn Off Worry

By the end of this chapter ...
   You will know how to:

- Distract yourself from obsessive worry

- Use thought-stopping to disrupt worry

- Postpone your worry

- Develop an effective plan to deal with worry

Lost in the Worry Spiral

Obsessive worry often becomes a negative spiral that can easily end in anxiety. When you're locked in a spiral of obsessive worry, you tend to ruminate on every facet of a perceived danger until it eclipses all other thoughts and you feel trapped. On a physiological and psychological level, anxiety becomes the next logical step—the natural response to the feeling of your mind spinning out of control. Because obsessive worry can be very compelling, it takes a deliberate act of will to break out of it. You need to make a concerted effort to move away from the mental vortex of worry and shift to another mode of thought.

Following the path of least resistance is likely to keep you spiraling until your anxiety symptoms take hold. Getting "out of your head" by doing or focusing on something outside yourself is an excellent way to halt the worry spiral. Although deliberately choosing to break out of obsessive worry may be difficult at first, with practice it gets easier.

Distracting Yourself from Worry

Pulling yourself out of the worry spiral requires a change of focus from the cerebral to the practical. You need to become engaged in a project or activity so that your concentration shifts from your fears of a possible, future danger to your strategies for completing the task at hand. Below is a list of ways to do this.

Do Physical Exercise

This can be your favorite exercise or sport, or just a household chore. If you don't want to have an exercise session, take a look around the house or office. What needs to be done? Do you have a project you've been putting off for a while? It can be as mundane as changing shelf paper or waxing the floor. Most people have an unwritten, long-term to-do list of projects around the house. Take a look at yours and see what needs to be done.

Talk to Someone

The modern world has sharply curtailed the amount of time we spend in conversation. Technology, the fast pace of contemporary life, and a general trend toward isolation have limited the time we devote not only to deep, meaningful conversations, but even everyday, simple chatting. Conversation is a great way to shift your focus away from your worries.

Generally, you should talk about something other than your worries, unless you want to express your feelings about them.

Do Twenty Minutes of Deep Relaxation

Your body is usually tense when you are stuck in worry. If you take time out to practice a relaxation technique, you'll often find your mind will tend to let go of whatever you were stuck on. Longer periods of relaxation (fifteen to twenty minutes) work better than short periods. You can use progressive muscle relaxation, a guided visualization, or meditation as described in chapters 1 and 2 to induce a state of deep relaxation.

Listen to Evocative Music

Feelings like sadness and anger may underlie and drive obsessive worrying. Music has a powerful ability to release these feelings. Take a look at your music collection and find a song or a whole CD that unlocks emotions for you. Many people find that, without consciously intending to, they've assembled an eclectic selection of music that they pick and choose from according to their mood. If this is true for you, take advantage of it to cut short the worry spiral.

Experience Something Immediately Pleasurable

You cannot be worried and feel comfortable and pleasant at the same time. Fear and pleasure are incompatible experiences. Anything you find pleasurable, whether it be a good meal, a warm bath, a funny movie, a back rub, cuddling, sexual activity, or simply walking in a beautiful setting, can help to move you away from worry and fearful thinking.

Use Visual Distractions

Simply look at something that absorbs your attention. This can be TV, movies, video games, your computer, uplifting reading, or even a rock garden.

Express Your Creativity

It's difficult to worry when you're being creative. Try arts and crafts, playing an instrument, painting or drawing, gardening, or simply rearranging your living room. If you have a hobby, spend some time working on it. Is there something you always wanted to try, like making jewelry or watercolor painting? This is an opportune time to begin new and rewarding activities.

Find an Alternative Positive Obsession

You can swap your negative obsession for a positive one by working on something that requires focused, steady concentration. For example, work out a crossword or jigsaw puzzle.

Repeat an Affirmation

A healthy ritual can be to sit quietly and practice repeating a positive affirmation that has personal significance. Repeat the affirmation slowly and deliberately. When your mind gets distracted, bring it back to the affirmation. Keep this up for five to ten minutes, or until you're fully relaxed. If you're spiritually inclined, some possible affirmations include:

• Let go and let God

• I abide in Spirit (God)

• I release (or turn over) this negativity to God

If you prefer a nonspiritual tack, try:

• Let it go

• These are just thoughts—they're fading away

- I'm whole, relaxed, and free of worry

Thought-Stopping

Sometimes you may find yourself stuck in a spiral of worrisome thoughts that just won't go away. They continue to loop in your head out of control. Thought-stopping is a time-honored technique for dealing with this kind of situation. It involves concentrating on an unwanted thought for a short time, then suddenly stopping it and emptying your mind. One of the oldest cognitive techniques still commonly practiced, thought-stopping was introduced by J. A. Bain in 1928 in his book *Thought Control in Everyday Life.* In the late 1950s it was adapted by Joseph Wolpe and other behavior therapists for the treatment of obsessive and phobic thoughts. With repeated practice, it becomes increasingly effective.

Exercise: Thought-Stopping

1. If you are alone and want to disrupt a chain of anxious thoughts, shout in a loud, forceful, and abrupt manner, "Stop!" "Stop it!" or "Get out!" Remember, you're trying to halt the spiral of worrisome thoughts. If others are around, shout internally, visualizing a large stop sign. You may also want to put a rubber band around your wrist and snap it as you shout.

2. Repeat step 1 several times, if necessary.

3. Every time the worrisome thoughts return, repeat your verbal command forcefully. When you succeed in extinguishing worry on several occasions with the shouted command, begin interrupting thoughts you don't want in your normal speaking voice. Eventually, with repeated practice, you may be able to disrupt your unwanted thoughts with a whispered or subvocal command to stop.

4. After having disrupted worrisome thinking by repeating the command to stop a few times, follow up with any of the distraction techniques listed in the section "Distracting Yourself from Worry" above.

Postpone Your Worry

Rather than trying to stop worry or obsessive thoughts altogether, you may opt to try postponing them for a bit. This strategy can be especially helpful when your attempt to stop worry abruptly (as in thought-stopping) feels like an uphill battle. In a sense, you pay some credence to your worries or obsessive thoughts by telling them that you will only ignore them for a few minutes and then attend to them again. In that way you avoid a fight with the part of your mind that seems compelled to worry or obsess.

When you first try this technique, try postponing worry only for a short time, perhaps two or three minutes. Then, at the end of the allotted time, try postponing again for a short time. When that period of time is up, set another specified time to postpone your obsessive thoughts. The trick is to keep postponing worry for as long as you can. Often you will be able to postpone a particular worry long enough that your mind moves on to something else. The worry just loses its strength, the longer you postpone it. For example, suppose you're trying to get work done and a worry about how you're going to pay all of your expenses keeps entering your mind. Accept the worry, without trying to fight with it, but tell yourself you'll postpone thinking about it for five minutes. After five minutes is up, tell yourself that you're going to postpone thinking about your worry for another five minutes. And so on.

When you're first trying out this technique, work with short periods of postponement such as one to five minutes. After you gain proficiency with it, try postponing for longer periods from an hour up to a day. If, after postponing worry two or three times, you feel you just can't postpone it any longer, give yourself five or ten minutes of worry time. That is, deliberately focus on the worry for a short period of time. At the end of the time, try to postpone again. If you're having difficulty with continuing to postpone, then utilize the basic distraction and thought-stopping techniques described earlier in this chapter.

Postponing worry is a skill that you can improve with practice. As with the other worry-stopping techniques, gaining skill with worry-postponement will increase your confidence in your ability to handle all kinds of worries and obsessive thoughts.

Plan Effective Action to Deal with Worry

Worrying about getting through a job interview, making a speech, or taking a long flight can be more stressful than the actual experience. That's because your body's fight-or-flight system makes no distinction between your fantasies about the situation and the situation itself. Worrying about an imagined danger causes your muscles to tighten and your stomach to churn just as much as when you're faced with a real danger. When you feel stuck in a particular worry, a useful strategy is to develop a plan of action to deal with the worry. The simple process of developing such a plan will divert your mind away from the worry. It will also help replace any sense of victimization you might be feeling with a more optimistic, hopeful attitude.

Exercise: Make a Plan to Deal with Your Worry

Think about what worries you the most. Is it money? Your relationship? Your kids? Your problem with anxiety itself? An upcoming performance situation? Among your worries, which one has highest priority for you to take action on right now? If you are ready and willing to take action, follow the sequence of steps below, adapted from *The Worry Control Workbook* by Mary Ellen Copeland (1998).

1. Write down the particular situation that is worrying you.

2. Make a list of possible things you can do to deal with and improve the situation. Write them down, even if they seem overwhelming or impossible to you right now. Ask family and friends for ideas as well. Don't judge any possible options at this point—simply write them down.

3. Consider each idea. Which ones are not possible? Which ones are doable but difficult to implement? Put a question mark after these. Which ones could you do in the next week to month? Put a check after these.

4. Make a contract with yourself to do all the things you checked off. Set specific dates for having them completed. When you have completed the checked items, go on to the more difficult things. Make a similar contract with yourself to do them.

5. Are there any other items that originally looked impossible that you might be able to do now? If so, make a contract with yourself to do these too.

6. Once you've fulfilled all of your contracts, ask yourself how the situation has changed. Has your worry been satisfactorily resolved? If the situation has not resolved, go through this process again.

If you continue to have problems with this worry, perhaps you have some self-limiting thought patterns or beliefs that are getting in your way. To understand and modify your personal belief system, see chapter 10 of *The Anxiety and Phobia Workbook* (Bourne 2000), "Mistaken Beliefs," and chapter 10 of *Beyond Anxiety and Phobia* (Bourne 2001), "Create Your Vision."

10

Cope on the Spot

By the end of this chapter …
  You will know how to:

- Use coping strategies and statements to combat anxiety
- Use affirmations to counter negative thoughts that fuel anxiety

Lean into Your Anxiety

Resisting or fighting anxiety is likely to make it worse. It's important to avoid tensing up in reaction to anxiety or trying to make it go away. Attempting to suppress or run away from the initial symptoms of anxiety is a way of telling yourself "I can't handle it." A more constructive approach is to cultivate an attitude that says, "Okay, here it is again. I can allow my body to go through its reactions and handle this. I've done it before." Acceptance of anxiety symptoms is the key. By cultivating an attitude of acceptance in the face of anxiety, you allow it to move through and pass. Anxiety is caused by a sudden surge of adrenaline. If you can let go and allow your body to have its reactions (such as heart palpitations, chest constriction, sweaty palms, and dizziness) caused by this surge, it will pass soon. Most of the adrenaline released will be metabolized and reabsorbed within five minutes. As soon as this happens, you'll start to feel better. Anxiety reactions are time limited. In most cases, anxiety peaks and begins to subside within a few minutes. Some anxiety may persist for a while, but the worst is over in a short time. It will pass more quickly if you don't aggravate it by fighting against it or reacting to it with fearful self-talk beginning with "what if ... "

But Know When to Marshal Your Defenses

Acceptance of the initial symptoms of anxiety is very important, but then it's time to do something. Anxiety and worry are passive states where you feel vulnerable, out of control, or even paralyzed. If you stand still and do nothing, your anxiety may tend to maintain itself or even build, leaving you feeling victimized. When anxiety comes on, always accept it first, then realize that there are many things you can actively do to redirect the energy spent on the anxiety into something constructive. In short, don't try to fight with anxiety, but don't do nothing either.

Taking Constructive Action: What to Do

To cope with anxiety in the moment, there are three types of recommended activities:

Coping strategies, which are active techniques to offset anxiety or distract yourself from it.

Coping statements, which are mental techniques designed to redirect your mind away from and replace fearful self-talk.

Affirmations, which can be used much like coping statements but are intended to work over a longer time period. Coping strategies and statements help to get you through a particular episode of anxiety, while affirmations work with changing your core beliefs. For example, you could use a particular coping strategy or statement to get through a difficult situation, and you could also bring to mind an affirmation about freedom from fear you have been working with for months.

Coping Strategies

A number of coping strategies have been covered in previous chapters. When faced with the onset of anxiety or worry, you can:

- Do something to *relax your body* (chapter 1). Abdominal breathing is often effective in offsetting acute anxiety. Try also slowing down whatever you're doing.

- Do something to *relax your mind* (chapter 2). Take fifteen or twenty minutes to do a guided visualization or to meditate.

- Take active steps to face your fear (chapter 4).

- Take time to self-nurture (chapter 7). Pleasurable activities such as talking to a friend, eating a good meal, taking a warm bath, or getting a back rub can be quite helpful.

- Distract yourself from a worry (chapter 9).

- Plan effective action to deal with a worry (chapter 9).

Beyond these, there are other active coping strategies that you might find helpful in dealing with all levels of anxiety from worry and mild apprehension to panic. Some of the most popular strategies are described below.

Talk to a Supportive Person Nearby or on the Phone

Talking to someone will help you to get your mind off your anxious body symptoms and thoughts. Whether you are driving in a car (with a passenger or a cell phone), standing in line at the grocery store, standing in an elevator, or flying in a plane, this can work very well. In a public-speaking situation, confiding in your audience can often help to dispel initial anxiety.

Move Around or Engage in Some Routine Activity

Moving and doing something physical lets you dissipate the extra energy or adrenaline created by the fight-or-flight reaction that occurs during acute anxiety. Instead of resisting the normal physiological arousal that accompanies anxiety, you move with it. At work you can walk to the bathroom and back or walk outdoors for ten minutes. At home you can do household chores requiring physical activity or work out on your stationary bike or rebounder. Gardening is an excellent way to channel the physical energy of an anxiety reaction.

Stay in the Present

Focus on concrete objects around you in your immediate environment. In a grocery store, for example, you might look at the people standing around or the various magazines next to the cash register. While driving, you might focus on the cars in front of you or on the other details of the surrounding environment (so long as you don't look away from the highway, of course). Staying in the present and focusing on external objects will help minimize the attention you give to troublesome physical symptoms or catastrophic "what-if" thoughts. If possible, you might try actually touching objects nearby to reinforce staying in the immediate present. Another good way to ground yourself is to focus on your legs and feet. As you're standing or walking, pay attention to your legs and feet and imagine that you are connected to the ground.

Simple Distraction Techniques

There are many simple, repetitive acts that can help distract your attention away from your anxiety. You can:

- Unwrap and chew a piece of gum

- Count backward from 100 in threes: 100, 97, 94, and so on

- Count the number of people in line (or all of the lines) at the grocery store

- Count the money in your wallet

- While driving, count the bumps on the steering wheel

- Snap a rubber band on your wrist. This may jar your mind out of anxious thoughts

- Take a cold shower

- Sing

See the section "Distracting Yourself from Worry" in chapter 9 for further suggestions on distraction.

Note: Distraction techniques are fine for helping you cope with the sudden onset of anxiety or worry. However, don't let distraction become a way of avoiding or running away from your anxiety. Ultimately, you need to directly experience anxiety and let it pass, in order to habituate to it. Every time you experience a surge of anxiety and allow it to pass without trying to get away from it, you learn that you can survive whatever your nervous system dishes out. In so doing, you build confidence in your ability to manage your anxiety in any and all situations.

Get Angry with Anxiety

Anger and anxiety are incompatible responses. It's impossible to experience both at the same time. In some cases it turns out that symptoms of anxiety are a stand-in for deeper feelings of anger, frustration, or rage. If you can get angry at your anxiety the moment it arises, you may stop it from building any further. You can do this either verbally or physically. You might say things to your symptoms such as: *Get out of my way. I have things to do! To hell with this—I don't care what other people think! This reaction is ridiculous—I'm going into this situation anyway!* This approach of "doing it to the anxiety before it does it to you" can be effective for some people.

Time-honored techniques for physically expressing anger include:

- Pounding on a pillow on your bed with both fists

- Screaming into a pillow—or in your car alone with the windows rolled up

- Hitting a bed or a couch with a plastic baseball bat

- Throwing eggs into the bathtub (the remains wash away)

- Chopping wood

Please keep in mind that it's very important in expressing anger to direct it either into empty space or toward an object, *not at another person.* If you find yourself quite angry with someone, vent the physical charge of your anger first in one of the above ways before you attempt to communicate with that person. Rise above physical and verbal expressions of anger toward other human beings, especially those you love and care about.

Experience Something Immediately Pleasurable

Just as anger and anxiety are incompatible responses, so the feeling of pleasure is incompatible with an anxiety state.

Any of the following may help to offset anxiety, worry, or even panic:

- Have your significant other or spouse hold you (or give you a back rub)
- Take a hot shower or relax in a hot bath
- Have a pleasurable snack or meal
- Engage in sexual activity
- Read humorous books or watch a comical video

Try a Cognitive Shift

Thinking about any of the following ideas may help you to shift your point of view so that you can let go of worry or anxious thoughts:

- Acknowledge that it would be okay to lighten up about this.
- Turn the problem over to your Higher Power.
- Trust in the inevitability of it passing. Affirm "this too will pass."
- Realize that it's not likely to be as bad as your worst thoughts about it.
- Realize that working with the problem is part of your path to healing and recovery.
- Remember not to blame yourself. You're doing your best, and that's the best anyone can do.
- Expand your compassion for all people who experience similar anxiety. Remember you're not alone.

Coping Statements

Coping statements are designed to redirect—and retrain—your mind away from fearful, "what-if" self-talk toward a more confident and comfortable stance in response to anxiety. When you're anxious, you're highly suggestible and thus more susceptible to what-if statements your mind brings up. If you suggest to yourself more supportive, realistic, and calming statements, your mind will begin to accept these ideas instead. *With repeated practice over time, you'll eventually internalize your coping statements to the point that they automatically come to mind when you find yourself confronted with anxiety or worry.* There are three kinds of coping statements:

1. coping statements for planning in advance to face a difficult situation

2. coping statements to use when first confronting a difficult or fearful situation

3. coping statements to offset uncomfortable sensations of anxiety or panic (whether they occur spontaneously or in facing a difficult situation)

Coping Statements for Preparing to Face a Fearful Situation

Today I'm willing to go just a little outside my comfort zone.

This is an opportunity for me to learn to become comfortable with this situation.

Facing my fear of _____ is the best way to overcome my anxiety about it.

Each time I choose to face _____, I take another step toward becoming free of fear.

By taking this step now, I'll eventually be able to do what I want.

There's no right way to do this. Whatever happens is fine.

I know I'll feel better once I'm actually in the situation.

Whatever I do, I'll do the best I can.

I praise myself for being willing to confront my fear of
_____.

There's always a way to retreat from this situation if I
need to.

Coping Statements for Entering a Fearful Situation

I've handled this before and I can handle it now.

Relax and go slowly. There's no need to push right now.

Nothing serious is going to happen to me.

It's okay to take my time with this. I'll do only as much as
I'm ready to do today.

I'm going to be all right. I've succeeded with this before.

I don't have to do this perfectly. I can let myself be
human.

I can think about being in a peaceful place as I undertake
this.

I can monitor my anxiety level and retreat from this situation if I need to.

Coping Statements for Feelings of Being Trapped

Just because I can't leave right now doesn't mean I'm
trapped. I'll relax for now, then leave in awhile.

The idea of being trapped is just a thought. I can relax and
let go of that thought.

General Coping Statements for Anxiety or Panic

I can handle these symptoms or sensations.

These sensations (feelings) are just a reminder to use my coping skills.

I can take my time and allow these feelings to pass.

I deserve to feel okay right now.

This is just adrenaline—it will pass in a few minutes.

This will pass soon.

I can ride this through.

These are just thoughts—not reality.

This is just anxiety—I'm not going to let it get to me.

This anxiety won't hurt me, even if it doesn't feel good.

Nothing about these sensations or feelings is dangerous.

I don't need to let these feelings and sensations stop me. I can continue to function.

This isn't dangerous.

These are just (anxious) thoughts—nothing more.

So what.

Put Your Coping Statements on Cards

So that your coping statements are readily available, it's a good idea to put your favorite ones on an index card (or several cards, if you prefer), which you can keep in your purse or wallet, or tape to the dashboard of your car. Whenever you feel symptoms of anxiety coming on, bring out the card and read it. *Remember, you need to practice your coping statements many times before you'll fully internalize them.* Eventually, they will take the place of the fearful, catastrophic self-talk that tends to keep your anxiety going. The effort you put into practicing coping statements will be well worth it.

Affirmations

Coping statements, along with the coping strategies discussed earlier, can help diminish anxiety in the moment. Affirmations can be in the moment, but are also useful over the long term. They can help you to change long-standing beliefs which tend to perpetuate anxiety. Their purpose is to help you cultivate a more constructive and self-empowering attitude toward your own experience of anxiety. Instead of being a passive victim of anxiety, you can cultivate an attitude of active mastery. Instead of feeling helplessly stuck or overwhelmed by panic, fearfulness, or worry, you can cultivate an attitude of greater confidence and faith in your ability to overcome your anxiety.

The following affirmations are intended to help you change the core attitudes and beliefs that contribute to your anxiety. Reading through them once or twice won't make much difference. Rehearsing them daily for a few weeks or months, however, will begin to help you change your basic outlook about fear in a constructive direction. One way to do this is to read through the list slowly once or twice each day. Think about each statement as you read it. Even better, record the list on audio tape, leaving a few seconds of silence between each affirmation. Then listen to the tape once daily, when relaxed, to reinforce a more positive and confident attitude about yourself and your life.

Negative Thoughts and Positive Affirmations to Combat Them

This is unbearable.
I can learn how to cope better with this.

What if this goes on without letting up?
I'll deal with this one day at a time. I don't have to project into the future.

I feel damaged, inadequate relative to others.
Some of us have steeper paths to walk than others. That

doesn't make me less valuable as a human being—even if I accomplish less in the outer world.

Why do I have to deal with this? Other people seem freer to enjoy their lives.
Life is a school. For whatever reasons, at least for now, I've been given a steeper path—a tougher curriculum. That doesn't make me wrong. In fact, adversity develops qualities of strength and compassion.

Having this condition seems unfair.
Life can appear unfair from a human perspective. If we could see the bigger picture, we'd see that everything is proceeding according to plan.

I don't know how to cope with this.
I can *learn* to cope better, step by step—with this and any difficulty life brings.

I feel so inadequate relative to others.
Let people do what they do in the outer world. I'm following a path of inner growth and transformation, which is at least equally valuable. Finding peace in myself can be a gift to others.

Each day seems like a major challenge.
I'm learning to take things more slowly. I make time to take care of myself. I make time to do small things to nurture myself.

I don't understand why I'm this way—why this happened to me.
The causes are many, including heredity, early environment, and cumulative stress. Understanding causes satisfies the intellect, but it's not what heals.

I feel like I'm going crazy.
When anxiety is high, I *feel* like I'm losing control. But that feeling has nothing to do with going crazy. Anxiety disorders are a long way from the category of disorders labeled "crazy."

I have to really fight this.
Struggling with a problem won't help as much as making more time in my life to better care for myself.

I shouldn't have let this happen to me.
The long-term causes of this problem lie in heredity and childhood environment, so I didn't cause this condition. I *can* now take responsibility for getting better.

Antianxiety Affirmations

I am learning to let go of worry.

Each day I'm growing in my capacity to master worry and anxiety.

I am learning not to feed my worries—to choose peace over fear.

I am learning to consciously choose what I think, and I choose thoughts that are supportive and beneficial for me.

When anxious thoughts come up, I make time to relax and release them.

Deep relaxation gives me the freedom of choice to move out of fear.

Anxiety is made of illusory thoughts—thoughts I can let go of.

When I see most situations as they truly are, there is nothing to be afraid of.

Fearful thoughts are usually exaggerated, and I'm growing in my ability to turn them off at will.

More and more, it's becoming easier to relax and talk myself out of anxiety.

I keep my mind too busy thinking positive and constructive thoughts to have much time for worry.

I'm learning to control my mind and choose the thoughts that I think.

I am gaining more confidence in myself, knowing I can handle any situation that comes along.

Fear is dissolving and vanishing from my life. I am calm, confident, and secure.

As I take life more slowly and easily, I have more ease and peace in my life.

As I grow in my ability to relax and feel secure, I realize that there is truly nothing to fear.

More and more, I'm growing in confidence, knowing that I can handle any situation that comes up.

Script for Overcoming Fear

The following script works well when recorded on audiotape. Remember to read it slowly.

Focusing on a fear always makes it worse. When I can relax enough, I become able to change my focus ... I can put my mind on loving, supportive, constructive ideas. I can't make fearful thoughts go away. Struggling with them makes them loom larger. Instead, I can redirect my mind to more peaceful, calming thoughts and circumstances. Every time I do this, I am choosing peace instead of fear. The more I choose peace, the more it becomes a part of my life. With practice, I get better at redirecting my mind. I learn how to spend less time focusing on fear. I grow stronger in my ability to choose wholesome, helpful thoughts over fearful ones. I make time to relax ... to reconnect with that place deep within myself that is always at peace.

When I make the time to do this, I can choose to move away from fearful thoughts. I can allow my mind to expand into a wider place that is much larger than my fearful thoughts. Fear requires a narrow, small focus of my mind. When I relax or meditate, my mind becomes deep enough—and large enough—to transcend fear. I'm learning to see that my fearful thoughts grossly exaggerate risk or threat. The true risk I face in most situations is actually very small. Of course, it's impossible to eliminate risk from life altogether. Being in a physical body in the physical world necessitates some risk. Only in heaven is there an eternal risk-free state. Right now, I'm learning to recognize my tendency to exaggerate risks—to blow them out of proportion. Every fear involves both overestimating the risk of danger and underestimating my ability to cope. If I take the time to examine my fearful thoughts, I'll discover that in most cases they are unrealistic. When I choose to see most situations as they truly are, I see that they are not dangerous. If I practice replacing my fearful thoughts with real thoughts, eventually my fearful thoughts will diminish. Every time I feel afraid, I recognize the unreality of my fearful thoughts and let go of them more easily.

The important thing is not to feed fear ... not to dwell on it or give it energy. Instead I can practice redirecting my attention to something—anything— that makes me feel better. I can focus on talking to a friend, reading something uplifting, working with my hands, listening to a tape, or any number of activities which help me take my mind off fear. With practice, I become more and more adept at moving away from fearful thoughts and not indulging in them. I begin to become master rather than victim of my mind. I learn that I have more choice about fear. I can step into it or out of it. As time passes, I learn to step out of it. My life gains more ease and tranquility. In so doing, I contribute to a more peaceful world.

Resources

Further Reading on Anxiety

Antony, Martin, and Richard Swinson. 2000. *The Shyness and Social Anxiety Workbook*. Oakland, Calif.: New Harbinger Publications.

Beckfield, Denise F. 1998. *Master Your Panic and Take Back Your Life*. Second Edition. San Luis Obispo, Calif.: Impact Publishers.

Bourne, Edmund J. 1998. *Healing Fear*. New York: Fine Communications.

Bourne, Edmund J. 2000. *The Anxiety and Phobia Workbook*. Third Edition. Oakland, Calif.: New Harbinger Publications.

Bourne, Edmund J. 2001. *Beyond Anxiety and Phobia*. Oakland, Calif.: New Harbinger Publications.

Copeland, Mary Ellen. 1998. *The Worry Control Workbook*. Oakland, Calif.: New Harbinger Publications.

Feniger, Mani. 1998. *Journey from Anxiety to Freedom*. Rocklin, Calif.: Prima Publishers.

Foa, Edna, and Reid Wilson. 1991. *Stop Obsessing: How to Overcome Your Obsessions and Compulsions.* New York: Bantam.

Hyman, Bruce, and Cherry Pedrick. 1999. *The OCD Workbook.* Oakland, Calif.: New Harbinger Publications.

Rapee, Ronald. 1998. *Overcoming Shyness and Social Phobia.* Northvale, N.J.: Jason Aronson.

Ross, Jerilyn. 1994. *Triumph over Fear.* New York: Bantam.

Zeurcher-While, Elke. 1998. *An End to Panic.* Second Edition. Oakland, Calif.: New Harbinger Publications.

Books on Exercise

Brems, Marianne. 1987. *Swim for Fitness.* San Francisco: Chronicle Books.

Cooper, Kenneth H. 1977. *The Aerobic Way.* New York: M. Evans and Company.

Fixx, Jim F. 1980. *Jim Fixx's Second Book of Running.* New York: Random House.

Gale, Bill. 1979. *The Wonderful World of Walking.* New York: William Morrow.

Gaston, Eugene A., and David L. Smith. 1979. *Get Fit with Bicycling.* Emmaus, Pa.: Rodale Press.

Hittleman, Richard. 1983. *Yoga for Health.* New York: Ballantine Books.

Sorenson, Jacki. 1979. *Aerobic Dancing.* New York: Rawson Wade.

Spino, Mike. 1979. *Beyond Jogging: The Inner Space of Running.* New York: Pocket Books.

Thomas, Gregory S. 1981. *Exercise and Health: Evidence and Implications.* New York: Oelger, Shlager, Gunn & Hain.

Wiener, Harvey S. 1980. *Total Swimming.* New York: Simon & Schuster.

Books on Nutrition

Balch, James, and Phyllis Balch. 1997. *Prescription for Nutritional Healing.* Second Edition. Garden City Park, N.Y.: Avery Publishing Group.

Bender, Stephanie. 1989. *PMS: Questions and Answers.* Los Angeles: Price Sloan.

Bloomfield, Harold. 1998. *Healing Anxiety with Herbs.* New York: HarperCollins.

Cass, Hyla, and Terrence McNally. 1998. *Kava: Nature's Answer to Stress, Anxiety, and Insomnia.* Rocklin, Calif.: Prima Health.

Dufty, William F. 1993. *Sugar Blues.* New York: Warner Books.

Haas, Elson M. 1992. *Staying Healthy with Nutrition.* Berkeley, Calif.: Celestial Arts.

Mindell, Earl. 1979. *Vitamin Bible.* New York: Warner Books.

Mindell, Earl. 1992. *Herb Bible.* New York: Simon and Schuster/Fireside Books.

Robbins, John. 1987. *Diet for a New America.* Walpole, N.H.: Stillpoint Publishing.

Weil, Andrew. 1995. *Natural Health, Natural Medicine.* New York: Houghton Mifflin.

Weil, Andrew. 2001. *Eating Well for Optimum Health.* New York: Quill.

Wurtman, Judith. 1988. *Managing Your Mind and Mood through Food.* New York: Perennial Library.

Books to Help You Simplify Your Life

Eisenson, Marc, Gerri Detweiler, and Nancy Castleman. 2001. *Stop Junk Mail Forever.* Elizaville, N.Y.: Good Advice Press.

Elgin, Duane. 1993. *Voluntary Simplicity.* New York: William Morrow.

Fanning, Patrick, and Heather Garnos Mitchener. 2001. *The 50 Best Ways to Simplify Your Life.* Oakland, Calif.: New Harbinger Publications.

Mundis, Jerold. 1990. *How to Get Out of Debt, Stay Out of Debt, and Live Prosperously.* New York: Bantam Books.

Schecter, Harriet. 2000. *Let Go of Clutter.* New York: McGraw-Hill Trade.

St. James, Elaine. 1994. *Simplify Your Life.* New York: Hyperion.

Uplifting Books

Beattie, Melody. 1990. *The Language of Letting Go.* New York: Harper/Hazelden.

Bloch, Douglas. 1990. *Words That Heal.* New York: Bantam.

Borysenko, Joan. 1994. *Fire in the Soul.* New York: Warner Books.

Caddy, Eileen. 1996. *Opening Doors Within.* Forres, Scotland: Findhorn Press Ltd.

Chopra, Deepak. 1995. *The Seven Spiritual Laws of Success.* San Rafael, Calif.: Amber-Allen Publishing.

Hay, Louise. 1984. *You Can Heal Your Life.* Santa Monica, Calif: Hay House.

Jampolsky, Gerald. 1979. *Love Is Letting Go of Fear.* Berkeley, Calif.: Celestial Arts.

Miller, Carolyn. 1995. *Creating Miracles.* Tiburon, Calif.: H. J. Kramer, Inc.

Redfield, James. 1993. *The Celestine Prophecy.* New York: Warner Books.

Rodegast, Pat. 1985. *Emmanuel's Book.* New York: Bantam.

Roman, Sanya. 1989. *Spiritual Growth.* Tiburon, Calif.: H. J. Kramer.

Tolle, Eckhart. 1999. *The Power of Now.* Novato, Calif.: New World Library.

Walsch, Neale. 1996. *Conversations with God, Book 1.* New York: Putnam.

Williamson, Marianne. 1994. *Illuminata.* New York: Random House.

Zukav, Gary. 1990. *The Seat of the Soul.* New York: Fireside Books.

Relaxing Music

Selections from any of the following artists are recommended for their relaxing effect:

William Ackerman

Jim Brickman

Steve Halpern

Michael Jones

David Lanz

George Winston

In general, collections or samplers of music put together by Windham Hill or Narada are recommended.

For classical enthusiasts, we recommend *The Most Relaxing Classical Album in the World...Ever!* by Virgin Records.

CDs and audiotapes by the above artists can be found at Borders or Barnes and Noble Bookstores, or by going to Amazon.com, clicking on "popular music," and searching under the artist's name.

Web Sites

www.adaa.org

Web site of the Anxiety Disorders Association of America. Includes information for consumers and professionals, message boards, chats, and a directory of professionals by zip code.

www.algy.com/anxiety

Search engine for anxiety, panic, trauma, stress, obsessive-compulsive disorder, etc.

www.healingwell.com/anxiety

Web site of the Anxiety-Panic Resource Center. Basic information, newsletter, articles, personal experiences, message boards, and chat.

Additional Hierarchies

Groups

If helpful, do entire sequence first with a support person, and then eventually alone.

1. Join a small group of acquaintances and remain three to five minutes without participating.

2. Same as #1 but say something, if only giving your name.

3. Same as #1, but remain up to ten minutes, saying something briefly.

4. Same as #1, but stay in the group for at least ten minutes and speak up for one minute or engage in a brief conversation.

5. Same as #4, but lengthen time you stay in group up to a half-hour and time you speak up to five minutes.

6. Repeat steps 1-5 in a large group of people where you know a few persons.

7. Repeat steps 1-5 with a small group of strangers (your support person still present).

8. Repeat steps 1-5 with a large group of strangers (your support person still present).

9. Repeat steps 1-8 alone, without a support person.

Flying

Do the entire sequence first with a support person, and then eventually alone.

1. Approach the airport and drive around it

2. Park at the airport, enter the terminal, and remain one to ten minutes.

3. If possible (security provisions may prevent this), arrange to go sit at a gate for one to ten minutes.

4. If possible, arrange to stay in a grounded plane for five minutes.

5. Leave the grounded plane and then renter. This time have the door to the plane closed.

6. Complete a short flight, no more than 20-30 minutes duration.

7. Complete a longer flight, one to two hours duration.

8. Complete a long flight, three to five hours duration.

Steps 4 and 5 are usually part of formal fear of flying programs available at many major airports. If no such program is available, arrange to do this on a smaller plane at a private airport that offers flying lessons.

Shopping in a Supermarket

If helpful , do entire first sequence with a support person nearby or in the store, then with your support person sitting outside in the car, and then eventually alone.

1. Sit in the parking lot and look at the store.

2. Walk up to the door of the store and remain there for one to five minutes.

3. Walk in and out of the door to the store.

4. Walk in the door and remain in the front of the store for one to five minutes.

5. Walk halfway back into the store and remain for one to five minutes.

6. Walk to the back of the store and remain for one to five minutes.

7. Remain in the store from five to ten minutes, visiting various sections.

8. Remain in the store from ten to thirty minutes.

9. Purchase one item at the express checkout counter.

10. Purchase two or three items at the express checkout counter, with one or two people waiting ahead of you.

11. Purchase more than three items at the express checkout counter, with more than two people waiting ahead of you.

12. Purchase three or more items at a regular checkout counter.

13. Same as #12, but purchase five to ten items.

14. Same as #12 , but purchase ten to twenty items.

References

Bain, J. A. 1928. *Thought Control in Everyday Life*. New York: Funk and Wagnalls.

Benson, Herbert. 1975. *The Relaxation Response*. New York: William Morrow.

———. 1984. *Beyond the Relaxation Response*. New York: Times Books.

Bourne, Edmund J. 2000. *The Anxiety and Phobia Workbook*. Third Edition. Oakland, Calif.: New Harbinger Publications.

———. 2001. *Beyond Anxiety and Phobia*. Oakland, Calif.: New Harbinger Publications.

Copeland, Mary Ellen. 1998. *The Worry Control Workbook*. Oakland, Calif.: New Harbinger Publications.

Elgin, Duane. 1993. *Voluntary Simplicity*. New York: William Morrow.

Jacobson, Edmund. 1974. *Progressive Relaxation*. Chicago: The University of Chicago Press, Midway Reprint.

Sears, Barry. 1995. *The Zone*. New York: HarperCollins.

Wilson, Reid. 1996. *Don't Panic*. New York: HarperCollins.

Edmund J. Bourne, Ph.D., has specialized in the treatment of anxiety disorders and related problems for two decades. For many years, Bourne was director of the Anxiety Treatment Center in San Jose and Santa Rosa, California. His best-selling anxiety workbooks, which have helped hundreds of thousands of readers throughout the world, include *The Anxiety and Phobia Workbook* and *Beyond Anxiety and Phobia.* Bourne lives and practices in Hawaii and in California.

Lorna Garano is a freelance writer and editor living in Oakland, California.

Some Other New Harbinger Titles

Surviving Your Borderline Parent, Item 3287 $14.95

When Anger Hurts, second edition, Item 3449 $16.95

Calming Your Anxious Mind, Item 3384 $12.95

Ending the Depression Cycle, Item 3333 $17.95

Your Surviving Spirit, Item 3570 $18.95

Coping with Anxiety, Item 3201 $10.95

The Agoraphobia Workbook, Item 3236 $19.95

Loving the Self-Absorbed, Item 3546 $14.95

Transforming Anger, Item 352X $10.95

Don't Let Your Emotions Run Your Life, Item 3090 $17.95

Why Can't I Ever Be Good Enough, Item 3147 $13.95

Your Depression Map, Item 3007 $19.95

Successful Problem Solving, Item 3023 $17.95

Working with the Self-Absorbed, Item 2922 $14.95

The Procrastination Workbook, Item 2957 $17.95

Coping with Uncertainty, Item 2965 $11.95

The BDD Workbook, Item 2930 $18.95

You, Your Relationship, and Your ADD, Item 299X $17.95

The Stop Walking on Eggshells Workbook, Item 2760 $18.95

Conquer Your Critical Inner Voice, Item 2876 $15.95

The PTSD Workbook, Item 2825 $17.95

Hypnotize Yourself Out of Pain Now!, Item 2809 $14.95

The Depression Workbook, 2nd edition, Item 268X $19.95

Call toll free, **1-800-748-6273,** or log on to our online bookstore at **www.newharbinger.com** to order. Have your Visa or Mastercard number ready. Or send a check for the titles you want to New Harbinger Publications, Inc., 5674 Shattuck Ave., Oakland, CA 94609. Include $4.50 for the first book and 75¢ for each additional book, to cover shipping and handling. (California residents please include appropriate sales tax.) Allow two to five weeks for delivery.

Prices subject to change without notice.